ISBN – 978-1492817208
ISBN – 1492817201

To order additional books, call: 573-692-6051

For other books to enrich your life, visit:

 beaconofhopemin.org and click on Bible Truths Restored Publication to find spiritual books.

WRITTEN AND COMPILED BY: Deloris McQueen

Pastor Steven McQueen, Publishing Director
Editorial Director, Deloris McQueen

REVISED: September 22, 2013

Printed in the United States of America

Home Cook'n At It's Best

HOME COOK'N AT IT'S BEST

BIBLE TRUTHS RESTORED
PUBLICATIONS

TABLE OF CONTENTS

"...man shall not live by bread alone; but by every word that proceedeth out of the mouth of God."
Matthew 4:4

"Of course, you shall live by every recipe from this book as well; nothing like a good meal like momma use to fix, because nobody cooks like momma. I know you will find this book a unique one. I am sure these recipes will bless you as it has our family."

-Pastor Steven McQueen

KITCHEN BASICS

To ensure consistency in your cooking experience, it is very important to know how to accurately measure all your ingredients. First rule of thumb: Remember, not all measuring cups are the same, and that not all ingredients are measured the same. Some may not realize that there are specific measuring cups designed for measuring liquid and dry ingredients. And regardless if you realize it or not, they are not interchangeable. Saying this, if your recipes are not turning out like you would like them to. Maybe, it's not the recipe; it could be your measuring cups.

A liquid measuring cup is either glass or plastic with a handle. They come in various sizes, (1 cup, 2 cups, 4 cups, and even 8 cups). Your liquid measuring cups are not used just for water. You will also need them for: Honey, molasses, milk oils, and syrups.

A dry measuring cup is usually made from plastic or metal w/a handle. When using a dry measuring cup make sure you fill your ingredients to the rim of the cup. You may purchase these individually or as a set. The set comes with, ¼ cup, 1/3 cup, ½ cup and 1 cup sizes.

Dry measuring cups are not only used for flour and sugars. But for: shortening, sour cream, yogurt and even applesauce. These ingredients may not be "dry", but they mound when measured. Again, for an accurate measurement level at the top of the cup.

There are also, standards measuring spoons. They are used to measure both liquid and dry. You set will come in: ¼ teaspoon, ½ teaspoon, 1 teaspoon, and 1 tablespoon. Some sets may come with a 1/8 as well.

KITCHEN CONVERSION CHART

This...	Equals That...
1 tablespoon (tbsp)	3 teaspoons (tsp.)
1/16 cup	1 tbsp.
1/8 cup	2 tbsp.
1/6 cup	2 tbsp. + 2 tsp.
¼ cup	4 tbsp.
1/3 cup	5 tbsp. + 1 tsp.
3/8 cup	6 tbsp.
½ cup	8 tbsp.
2/3 cup	10 tbsp. + 2 tsp.
¾ cup	12 tbsp.
1 cup	48 tsp. or 16 tbsp.
8 fluid ounces (fl oz)	1 cup
1 pint (pt)	2 cups
1 quart (qt)	2 pts.
4 cups	1 qt.
1 gallon (gal)	4 qts.
16 ounces (oz)	1 pound (lb.)

Quantity	Small squares	100 gram tablets	20 gram bars
1 lb.	100	4½	23
1 oz.	6	6 small squares	1½
2 oz.	12	12 small squares	3
3 oz	19	19 small squares	4¼
4 oz	25	1 tablet + 4 small squares	5½
5 oz.	32	1 tablet + 11 small squares	7
6 oz.	38	1 + 17 small squares	8½
7 oz.	44	2 tablets + 2 small squares	10
8 oz.	50	2 tablets + 8 small squares	11½
9 oz.	57	2 tablets + 15 small squares	13
10 oz.	63	3 tablets	14
11 oz.	69	3 tablets + 6 small squares	15½
12 oz.	76	3 tablets + 13 small squares	17
13 oz.	82	3 tablets + 19 small squares	18½
14 oz.	88	4 tablets + 4 small squares	20
15 oz.	95	4 tablets + 11 small squares	21¼
16 oz. (1 lb.)	101	4 tablets + 17 small squares	22½

COOKING MEASUREMENT CONVERSION

Measurement	Equal To	
1 teaspoon (t.)	5 milliliters (ml)	
1 Tablespoon (T.)	3 t.	½ Fluid Ounce (fl.oz.)
1/8 Cup (C.)	2 T.	1 fl. oz.
¼ C.	4 T.	2 fl. oz.
1/3 C.	5 T. & 1 t.	1 ¾ fl. oz.
½ C.	8 T.	4 fl. oz.
2/3 C.	10 T. & 2 t.	3 ½ fl. oz.
¾ C.	12 T.	6 fl. oz.
1 C.	16 T.	8 fl. oz.
1 Pint	2 C.	16 fl. oz.
1 Quart	4 C.	2 pints
1 Liter	34 fl. oz.	
1 Gallon	16 C.	4 Quarts
1 Pound	454 Grams (g)	

CONVERSION FOR INGREDIENTS FREQUENTLY USED IN BAKING		
INGREDIENTS	OUNCES	GRAMS
1 cup all-purpose flour	5 ounces	142 grams
1 cup whole wheat flour	8 ½ ounces	156 grams
1 cup granulated (white) sugar	7 ounces	198 grams
1 cup firmly packed brown sugar	7 ounces	198 grams
1 cup powdered confectioner's sugar	4 ounces	113 grams
1 cup cocoa powder	3 ounces	85 grams

Butter
  4 tablespoons = ½ stick = 1/4 cup
  8 tablespoon = 1 stick = ½ cup
	2 ounces
	4 ounces
		57 grams
		113 grams

COOKIES AND MUFFINS

NO BAKE COOKIES

¼ Cup Cocoa
3 Cups Quick Oats
½ Cup Butter
½ Cup Peanut Butter
2 Cups Sugar
1 Tsp. Vanilla
½ Cup Milk

Bring to a rolling boil and continue to boil for 1 minute, (soft ball stage), remove from heat and add: oats, peanut butter and vanilla. Stir until well blended then drop by Tablespoon onto foil or wax paper and let cool.

BROWNIES

¼ Cup Butter
1 ¼ Cups Flour
2/3 Cup Shortening
1 Tsp. Vanilla
¾ Cup Cocoa
1 Tsp. Baking Powder
2 Cups Sugar
½ Tsp. Salt
4 Eggs
½ Cup Nuts (optional)

Melt butter, shortening and cocoa over low heat in a medium sauce pan. Combine sugar, flour vanilla, baking powder, salt and nuts in a bowl then stir in melted chocolate mixture until well blended. Pour into a 9x13 pan and bake at 350 degrees for 30-35 minutes.

MAGIC COOKIE BARS

½ Cup Butter
6 oz. Chocolate Chips
1 ½ Cup Graham
½ Cup Coconut
Cracker Crumbs
1 Cup Chopped Nuts
1 Can condensed Milk

In 9x13 baking pan melt butter. Remove from heat and sprinkle graham cracker crumbs evenly over butter. Pour milk over crumbs, layer with chocolate chips, coconut and nuts; press down gently then bake at 350 degrees for 25 minutes or until golden brown; Cool and cut into bars.

MOIST JUMBO RAISIN COOKIES

2 Cups Raisins
1 ½ Tsp. Cinnamon
1 Cup Water
¼ Tsp. Nutmeg
1 Cup Margarine
1 Tsp. Vanilla
3 Eggs
1 Tsp. Baking Powder
2 Cups Sugar
1 Tsp. Baking Soda
4 Cups Flour

Boil raisins in water for 5 minutes and let cool. Mix rest of ingredients then add raisins; drop by spoonful onto cookie sheet and bake at 350 for 10-12 minutes or until light brown.

YULETIDE LAYER BARS

½ Cup Butter
1 Can Condensed Milk
1 ½ Cups Graham
1 2/3 Cups Holiday Morsels (Nestlé's)
Cracker Crumbs
1 ½ Cups Coconut
1 Cup Chopped Nuts

PREHEAT oven to 350. Melt butter in 9x13 pan; remove from oven. Sprinkle graham cracker crumbs over butter. Stir well; carefully press onto bottom of pan. Sprinkle with coconut and nuts. Pour sweetened condensed milk evenly over top. Sprinkle with morsels; press down lightly. Bake for 25 to 30 minutes or until light golden brown. Cool and cut into bars.

HOLIDAY CHOCOLATE CHIP COOKIES

2 ¼ Cups Flour
¾ Cup packed Brown Sugar
1 Tsp. Baking Soda
1 Tsp. Vanilla Extract
1 Tsp. Salt
2 Eggs
1 Cup Butter (softened)
1 2/3 Cups Holiday Morsels
¾ Cup Sugar
1 Cup Chopped Nuts

PREHEAT oven to 350. Combine flour, baking soda and salt in a small bowl. Beat butter, sugar, brown sugar and vanilla in large mixer bowl until creamy. Add eggs one at a time, beating well after each addition. Gradually beat in flour mixture. Stir in 1 cup of morsels and nuts. Drop by rounded tablespoon onto ungreased baking sheets. Top with dollops of remaining morsels. Bake for 11 to 13 minutes or until golden brown. Coon on baking sheets on wire racks for 2 minutes; remove to wire racks to cool completely.

SNOW-TOPPED HOLIDAY BROWNIE BARS

1 Family Size Brownie Mix
1 Container White Frosting
1 2/3 Cup Holiday Morsels
Coconut (optional)

PREHEAT oven to 350 degrees. Grease 9x13 pan and prepare brownie mix according to directions. Spread batter into pan and sprinkle with 1 cup morsels. Bake according to package then cool on wire rack. Spread frosting over brownies and sprinkle with remaining morsels and coconut. Cut into bars.

APPLESAUCE COOKIES

½ Cup Shortening
1 ½ Tsp. Baking Soda
1 Cup Sugar

1 Tsp. Allspice
1 Egg Beaten
½ Tsp. Cinnamon
1 Cup Applesauce
½ Tsp. Nutmeg
½ Tsp. Salt
½ Cup Nuts

Stir in dry ingredients, raisins and nuts. Drop by teaspoonful and bake at 350 degrees until golden brown; Makes about 5 dozen.

PEANUT BUTTER COOKIES

¾ Cup Peanut Butter
1 ¾ Cup Flour
½ Cup Butter Flavor Crisco
1 Egg
1 ¼ Cup Brown Sugar
¾ Tsp. Salt
3 Tbsp. Milk
¾ Tsp. Baking Powder
1 Tbsp. Vanilla

PREHEAT oven to 375 degrees. Mix peanut butter, Crisco, brown sugar, vanilla and egg. Stir in flour, salt, baking powder and mix well. Drop by tablespoon on ungreased cookie sheet and bake 8-10 minutes.

CHOCOLATE CHIP COOKIES

¾ Cup Butter Flavor Crisco
¾ Tsp. Baking Soda
1 ¼ Cup Brown Sugar
1 Cup Chocolate Chips
2 Tbsp. Milk
1 Cup Chopped Pecans
1 Tbsp. Vanilla
1 ¾ Cups Flour
1 Egg
1 Tsp. Salt

PREHEAT oven to 375 degrees. Mix Crisco, brown sugar milk, vanilla and egg. Stir in flour, salt, baking soda, chocolate chips and nuts. Drop by tablespoon on ungreased cookie sheet and bake for 8-10 minutes for chewy cookies or 11-13 minutes for crisp cookies.

$1,000,000.00 CHOCOLATE CHIP COOKIES

2 Cups Butter
1 Tsp. Salt
2 Cups Sugar
2 Tsp. Baking Powder
2 Cups Brown Sugar
2 Tsp. Baking Soda
4 Eggs
24 Oz. Chocolate Chips
2 Tsp. Vanilla
1-8oz. Chocolate Bar (grated)
5 Cups Oats
3 Cups Chopped Nuts

Put oats in food processor until a fine powder. Cream Butter and sugars, add eggs and vanilla: mix in oats, salt, baking powder, baking soda; when well blended add: chocolate chips, grated chocolate bar and nuts. Roll into balls and place 2 inches apart on greased cookie sheet. Bake for 6-8 minutes at 375 degrees. Instead of the chocolate bar I substitute 8-10 oz. of Toblerone chocolate coarsely chopped.

MONSTER COOKIES

1 Lb. Margarine
3 (18 oz.) Jars Peanut Butter (Crunchy)
1 Dozen Eggs
8 Tsp. Baking Soda
2 Lb. Brown Sugar
18 Cups Quick Oats
4 Cups White Sugar
12 oz. Chocolate Chips
1 Tbsp. Vanilla
16 oz. M & M's
2 Tbsp. Karo Syrup

Use no flour in this recipe. Beat eggs, and then add all ingredients in given order in a large dishpan, adding oats last until quite stiff dough is formed. Slightly grease the cookie sheets. To make monster-size cookies, use an ice cream dipper, putting only 6 cookies per sheet. Bake in a 350 degree oven until

light brown. May be made into regular size cookies baking for 10-12 minutes or until light brown. These freeze well. Makes 30 pound lard can full.

DROP SUGAR COOKIES

2 Cups Flour
¾ Cup Sugar
2 Tsp. Baking Powder
2/3 Cup Vegetable Oil
½ Tsp. Salt
2 Tsp. Vanilla
2 Large Eggs
1 Tsp. Lemon Zest

PREHEAT oven to 400 degrees. Sift dry ingredients into a bowl, add all other ingredients and stir until well blended. Drop by teaspoonful on ungreased cookie sheet sprinkle with sugar and bake 8 minutes.

AMISH SUGAR COOKIES

1 Cup Sugar
4 ½ Cups Flour
1 Cup Powdered Sugar
1 Tsp. Baking Soda
1 Cup Butter
1 Tsp. Cream of Tartar
1 Cup Oil
1 Tsp. Vanilla
2 Eggs

Combine sugars, butter and oil; beat well. Add eggs and beat again. Add remaining ingredients and mix well. Drop small balls of dough on cookie sheet and flatten with a fork. Bake at 375 degrees for 10-12 minutes.

MOM'S BEST SUGAR COOKIES

1 Cup Butter
½ Cup Milk
2 Cups Sugar
5 Cups Flour
2 Eggs
2 Tsp. Baking Powder
1 Tsp. Vanilla
1 Tsp. Nutmeg

Cream together butter, sugar, eggs and vanilla, then add milk and mix. Sift flour with baking powder and nutmeg. Add to the creamed mixture reserving 1 cup flour mixture. Chill dough. When ready to bake, roll dough out on floured board using some of the reserved flour. Cut into desired shapes and bake at 350 degrees for 5-8 minutes. Let cool and decorate as desired.

WORLD'S BEST COOKIE

1 Cup Butter
1 Cup Crushed Corn Flakes
1 Cup Sugar
½ Cup Coconut
1 Cup Brown Sugar
½ Cup Chopped Nuts
1 Egg
3 ½ Cups Flour
1 Cup Oil
1 Tsp. Baking Soda
1 Tsp. Vanilla
1 Tsp. Salt
1 Cup Oats

Cream together butter and sugars until light and fluffy; Add egg mixing well, then add oil and vanilla and mix well. Add oats, corn flakes, coconut and nuts, flour baking soda and salt, mix well. Form into balls the size of walnuts. Place on ungreased cookie sheet and flatten (must flatten for proper texture). Bake at 325 degrees for 10-12 minutes; allow to cool on cookie sheet before removing.

SNICKERDOODLES

2 Cups Sugar (divided)
2 ¾ Flour
1 Cup Butter Flavor Crisco
2 Tsp. Cream of Tartar
2 Large Eggs
1 Tsp. Baking Soda
2 Tbsp. Milk
¾ Tsp. Salt
1 Tsp. Vanilla
2 Tsp. Cinnamon

PREHEAT oven to 400 degrees. Beat 1 ½ cups sugar, shortening, eggs, milk and vanilla in large bowl until well blended. Combine flour, cream of tartar, baking soda and salt in medium bowl then gradually add to shortening mixture, mixing just until blended. Combine remaining ½ cup sugar and cinnamon in small bowl. Shape dough into 1-inch balls and roll in sugar- cinnamon mixture. Place on baking sheets and bake 7-8 minutes. Remove to wire racks to cool. Makes 3 dozen cookies

MOLASSES COOKIES

¾ Cup Shortening
1 Tsp. Cinnamon
1 Cup Brown Sugar
1 Tsp. Ginger
1 Large Egg
½ Tsp. Cloves
¼ Cup Molasses
¼ Tsp. Salt
2 ¼ Cup Flour
¼ Cup Sugar
2 Tsp. Baking Soda

Preheat oven to 350 degrees. Combine shortening and brown sugar in large bowl and beat until well blended; add egg and molasses; beat until light and fluffy. Add flour, baking soda, cinnamon, ginger cloves and salt stir until well blended. Chill 3 hours or overnight. Shape in 1 inch balls; dip one side in sugar, place sugar side up on baking sheet and bake for 12 to 15 minutes. Cool on racks: Makes 4 dozen.

LITTLE WHITE COOKIES

1 cup butter (soft)
2 Cups Flour
½ Cup Powdered Sugar
¼ Tsp. Salt
2 Tsp. Vanilla
1 Cup Chopped Pecans

Preheat oven to 325 degrees. Mix all ingredients until well blended; form into balls and bake 15-20 minutes;

roll in powdered sugar while hot; let cool then roll again.

OATMEAL RAISIN COOKIES

1 Cup Shortening
2 Tsp. Baking Soda
1 Cup Sugar
1 Tsp. Salt
1 Cup Brown Sugar
1 Tsp. Cinnamon
3 Eggs
2 Cups Oats
1 Tsp. Vanilla
1 Cup Raisins
2 ½ Cups Flour
1 Cup Chopped Nuts

Preheat oven to 350 degrees. Cream together; shortening, sugar, brown sugar, vanilla and add eggs one at a time. Add dry ingredients and mix well. Make into balls and bake 10-11 minutes or until light brown. Makes 3 ½ dozen

OATMEAL COOKIES

1 ¾ Cups Flour
½ Cup Sugar
½ Tsp. Baking Soda
1 Egg
1 Tsp. Salt
½ Cup Buttermilk
½ Tsp. Cinnamon
¼ Cup Corn Syrup
¼ Tsp. Cloves
1 Tsp. Vanilla
¾ Cup Shortening
2 Cups Oats
1 Cup Brown Sugar
1 Cup Nuts

Preheat oven to 350 degrees. Cream together; shortening, brown sugar, sugar, egg, buttermilk, corn syrup and vanilla. Slowly add; flour, soda, salt, cinnamon, cloves, oats and nuts, mix until well

blended. Drop by tablespoon on ungreased cookie sheet and bake for 10-12 minutes or until light brown.

M & M COOKIES

2 Cups Flour
¾ Tsp. Baking Soda
¾ Tsp. Salt
1 Cup Butter
2/3 Cup Sugar
½ Cup Brown Sugar
1 Egg
1 Tsp. Vanilla
12 oz. Chocolate Chips
12 oz. M & M's

Mix sugar, brown sugar, egg, butter and vanilla. Add flour, soda, salt, chocolate chips and M&M's, stir until well blended. Drop by teaspoon onto ungreased cookie sheet and bake at 350 degrees for 10-12 minutes.

DUTCH COOKIES

½ Gallon Sorghum
2 Cups Lard or Shortening
½ Cup Baking Soda
1 Cup Buttermilk
2 Lbs. Dates
2 Lbs. Raisins
2 Cups Applesauce
2 Cups Brown Sugar
1 Tsp. Cinnamon
1 Tsp. Allspice
½ Tsp. Cloves
½ Tsp. Salt
1 Quart Pecans
8-10 Lbs. Flour

Combine lard or shortening with sorghum in large pan, heat until shortening is melted then remove from heat. Add soda and buttermilk and stir well; add dates and raisins that have been run through the food chopper. Add rest of ingredients and make into rolls and place in refrigerator overnight. Slice and bake at 350 degrees for 10 minutes.

SPRITZ COOKIES

1 Cup Butter or Margarine
1 Egg
¾ Cup Sugar
1 Tsp. vanilla
2 ¼ Cups Flour

Cream butter, sugar, vanilla and egg until blended. Gradually add flour. Drop by teaspoon onto ungreased cookie sheet and bake at 350 for 8 – 10 minutes.

OATMEAL BARS

¾ Cup Shortening
1 Cup Brown Sugar
½ Cup Sugar
¼ Cup Water
1 Tsp. Vanilla
1 Egg
1 Cup Flour
1 Tsp. Salt
½ Tsp. Baking Soda
3 Cups Oats
½ Cup Nuts
½ Cup Chocolate Chips
½ Cup Coconut

In a large bowl, combine the shortening, brown sugar, sugar, water vanilla and egg. Stir until fluffy. Add flour, salt and baking soda, mix well. Stir in oats, nuts, coconut and chocolate chips. Bake in a well-greased 9x13 pan at 350 degrees for 20 minutes or until done. Makes 24 bars.

DELICIOUS COOKIES

1 Cup Margarine
1 Tsp. Salt
1 Cup Oil
1 Tsp. Baking Soda
1 Cup Brown Sugar
1 Tsp. Cream of Tartar
1Cup White Sugar
1 Cup Oats
1 Egg

1 Cup Coconut
2 Tsp. Vanilla
1 Cup Rice Krispies
1 Tsp. Coconut Flavoring
6 oz. Chocolate Chips
3 ½ Cups Flour

Blend margarine and sugars; add oil, then egg and flavorings. Sift together the flour, salt, baking soda, cream of tartar and mix into the creamed mixture. Lastly, stir in the oats, coconut, Rice Krispies and chocolate chips. Drop onto lightly greased cookie sheet and bake about 12 minutes at 350 degrees until lightly browned. Makes about 6 dozen cookies

CHEWY CHOCOLATE COOKIES

1 ¼ Cups Butter
2 Cups Sugar
2 Eggs
2 Tsp. Vanilla
2 1/2 Cups Flour
¾ Cup Cocoa
1 Tsp. Baking Soda
½ Tsp. Salt
1 Cup Nuts Finely Chopped

Cream butter and sugar in larger mixer bowl. Add eggs and vanilla; blend well. Combine flour, cocoa, baking soda and salt into creamed mixture. Stir in nuts. Drop by teaspoon onto ungreased cookie sheet. Bake at 350 degrees for 8-9 minutes. (Do not over bake. Cookies will be soft. They will puff during baking, flatten upon cooling.) Cool on cookie sheet until set, about 1 minute; remove to wire rack to cool completely.

LEMON COOKIES

2 Cups Sugar
1 Cup Butter
2 Eggs
2 Tsp. Lemon Extract
3 Cups Flour
2 Tsp. Baking Powder
½ Tsp. Salt

Cream together Sugar and butter; add eggs and lemon extract; stir in flour, baking powder and salt until well mixed. Add nuts if you want. Drop on greased baking sheet and bake for 10 minutes at 350 degrees.

BLONDE BROWNIES

1 Cup Flour
1/3 Cup Butter
1/8 Tsp. Baking Soda
1 Cup Brown Sugar
½ Tsp. Baking Powder
1 Egg Beaten
½ Tsp. Salt
1 Tsp. Vanilla
½ Cup Nuts
½ Cup Chocolate Chips

Sift flour, soda, salt and baking powder; add nuts and mix well. Melt butter in saucepan; add brown sugar and mix well; add egg and vanilla; add to flour mixture; spread in 9 inch square pan, sprinkle chocolate chips on top and bake at 350 degrees for 20-25 minutes.

COCONUT COOKIES

1 Cup Shortening
¼ Tsp. Salt
1 ½ Cups Sugar
1 Tsp. Vanilla
2 Eggs
1 Cup Coconut
2 ¾ Cups Flour
2 Tbsp. Sugar
1 Tsp. Baking Soda
2 Tsp. Cinnamon

Cream shortening and sugar; add the eggs, flour, baking soda, salt, vanilla and coconut. Shape into balls and roll in the 2 Tablespoons of sugar and 2 Teaspoons of cinnamon that have been mixed together. Place on ungreased cookie sheet; flatten out with a fork and bake at 350 degrees for 8-10 minutes.

PEANUT BUTTER & JELLY COOKIES

1 Cup Peanut Butter
1 Cup Flour
½ Cup Butter
1 Tsp. Baking Soda
½ Cup Brown Sugar
1/8 Tsp. Salt
¼ Cup Sugar
1 Cup Grape Jelly
1 Egg

In a large mixing bowl, cream together peanut butter, brown sugar, butter and sugar; beat until smooth. Add Egg; mix thoroughly. In a separate bowl, combine flour, baking soda and salt. Gradually add to butter mixture, beating until well mixed. Cover and refrigcratc for 1 hour. Once dough has chilled, preheat oven to 375 degrees. Shape dough into 1 inch balls and place on ungreased cookie sheet; press a deep hole into the center of each ball with the handle of a wooden spoon. Bake 10-12 minutes or until lightly browned. Cool slightly before removing to cooling racks, and then fill the cookie indentation with grape jelly.

CHOCOLATE CHUNK & CHERRY COOKIES

1 ½ Cups Flour
2 Large Eggs
1 Cup Cocoa
2 Tsp. Vanilla
1 Tsp. Baking Soda
1 ½ Cups Bittersweet Chocolate (Chopped)
1 Tsp. Salt
1 Cup Butter
1 ½ Cups Dried Tart Cherries
1 ¼ Cup Brown Sugar
(May use figs-cranberries-apricots)

PREHEAT oven to 350 degrees. Combine flour, cocoa, baking soda and salt in a medium bowl; set aside. In a large bowl, mix butter and sugars until light and fluffy. Beat in the eggs one at a time and add vanilla. Reduce mixer speed to low and gradually add in the flour mixture until combined. Stir in the chopped chocolate and cherries. Shape 2 Tablespoons of dough into rough balls and place 2 inches apart on parchment lined baking sheet. Bake 11 – 13 minutes. Cool on the pan 2 minutes before transferring to wire rack.

SNICKER DELIGHTS

1 Cup Peanut Butter
3 Cups Flour
1 Cup Butter
½ Tsp. Salt
2 Tsp. Vanilla
1 Tsp. Baking Powder
2 Eggs
1 Tsp. Baking Soda
1 Cup Sugar
1 Bag Miniature Snickers
1 Cup Brown Sugar

Cut candy bars in ½ or if using snack size cut in 1/3. Mix butter, sugars, peanut butter, vanilla and eggs. Add flour, salt, soda and baking powder. Mix well. Chill. Wrap dough around snickers and make a ball. Place on ungreased baking sheet and bake at 350 degrees for 12-15 minutes or until golden brown; Let set for 2 minutes. Flatten each cookie lightly with a spatula; remove to wire rack to cool.

YUM YUM BARS

6 Cups Rice Krispies
1 Cup Light Corn Syrup
½ Cup Peanut Butter
12 oz. Chocolate Chips
1 Cup White Sugar
12 oz. Butterscotch Chips

Mix together Rice Krispies, peanut butter, white sugar and syrup. Press in buttered 9x13 pan and refrigerate. Melt together chocolate chips and butterscotch ships. Spread on top of Rice Krispies mixture and cut into bars.

RED VELVET COOKIES

6 Tbsp. Butter
1 Cup Powdered Sugar

1 Red Velvet Cake Mix
1 Tsp. Cornstarch
2 Large Eggs
1 Tsp. Lemon Zest

PREHEAT oven to 375 degrees. Melt butter; set aside to cool. Place powdered sugar and cornstarch in a small bowl. Mix with a fork to blend. Place cake mix, cooled butter, eggs and lemon zest in large mixing bowl. Mix by hand until well blended and a dough forms. Form dough into 1 inch balls and roll in powdered sugar mixture. Place on cool, ungreased cookie sheet, bake for 9-11 minutes until set. Cool 1 minute then transfer to wire rack to cool completely.

COCONUT MACAROONS

4 Egg Whites
2 2/3 Cup Coconut
2/3 Cup Sugar
¼ Cup Flour
½ Tsp. Vanilla
¼ Tsp. Salt
½ Tsp. Almond Extract

PREHEAT oven to 325 degrees. Stir together all ingredients in a large bowl, blending well. Drop dough by teaspoon onto lightly greased baking sheets. Bake for 18-20 minutes or until golden brown. Remove to wire racks to cool.

RANGER COOKIES

½ Cup Butter
½ Cup Sugar
½ Cup Brown Sugar
½ Tsp. Baking Powder
¼ Tsp. Baking Soda
1 Egg
1 Tsp. Vanilla
1 ¼ Cup Flour
2 Cups Crisp Rice Cereal
1 1/3 Cups Coconut
1 Cup Chopped Dates

PREHEAT oven to 375 degrees. In a large bowl combine brown sugar and butter with an electric mixer on medium for 30 seconds. Add granulated sugar, baking powder and baking soda. Beat until combined; scrapping side of bowl occasionally; beat in egg and vanilla until combined. Beat in as much of the flour as you can with the mixer; using a wooden spoon stir in any remaining flour, cereal coconut and dates. Drop by rounded teaspoon 2 inches apart on ungreased cookie sheets. Bake about 8 minutes or until edges are golden. Let stand on cookie sheets one minute. Transfer to wire racks and let cool. Makes about 54 cookies

GINGERSNAPS

2 ½ Cups Flour
½ Tsp. Cinnamon
½ Cup Shortening
½ Tsp. Nutmeg
½ Cup Sugar
¼ Tsp. Cloves
½ Cup Molasses
½ Tsp. Baking Soda
1 Egg Beaten
1 Tbsp. Hot Water
1 ½ Tsp. Ginger
1 Tsp. Vinegar

Sift flour, measure and resift. Cream shortening, blend in sugar and add molasses and egg; beat until smooth. Mix spices thoroughly with soda and blend until smooth with hot water and vinegar; stir into creamed mixture. Add flour, mixing thoroughly until smooth. Drop by teaspoon onto buttered baking sheet. Bake 10 minutes at 375 degrees. Remove to wire racks to cool. Makes 4-5 dozen cookies

PEANUT BRITTLE BARS

2 Cups Flour
½ Cup Brown Sugar
2/3 Cup Butter
2 Cups Cocktail Peanuts
1 Cup Milk Chocolate Pieces
12 oz. Jar Carmel Topping
3 Tbsp. Flour

PREHEAT oven to 350 degrees. Line a 15x10 baking pan with foil. Grease foil; set aside. In a medium bowl, stir together the 2 cups flour and the brown sugar. Using a pastry blender, cut in butter until mixture is crumbly. Press mixture onto bottom of prepared pan. Bake about 12 minutes or until golden. Sprinkle peanuts and milk chocolate pieces over top. In a small bowl, stir together caramel topping and the 3 tablespoons flour. Drizzle over top; Bake for 12 – 15 minutes more or until caramel is bubbly. Cool on a wire rack. Carefully lift foil; gently peel away from edges. Cut into bars. Makes 36 bars

ZUCCHINI COOKIES

1 Cup Sugar
1 Tsp. Cinnamon
½ Cup Butter
½ Tsp. Salt
1 Egg Beaten
1 Cup Grated Zucchini
2 Cups Flour
1 Cup Raisins
1 Tsp. Baking Soda
1 Cup Chopped Nuts
½ Tsp. Cloves

Cream sugar, butter and egg until fluffy and well blended; Sift dry ingredients together and add to mixture with grated zucchini, blending well. Stir in raisins and nuts. Drop by teaspoon on greased cookie sheet; Bake at 375 degrees for 12-15 minutes or until done. Do not over bake. Makes 3 dozen

FROSTED PUMPKIN COOKIES

1 Cup Shortening
1 Tsp. Baking Powder
1 Cup Sugar
1 Tsp. Baking Soda
1 Cup Pumpkin
1 Tsp. Salt
1 Tsp. Vanilla
1 Tsp. Cinnamon
1 Egg
½ Tsp. Ginger
2 Cups Flour

1 Cup Raisins
1 Cup Nuts

Cream shortening and sugar; add pumpkin, vanilla and egg. Stir to blend. Add dry ingredients and then raisins and nuts. Drop by teaspoon on cookie sheet. Bake 10-12 minutes at 350 degrees. Frost cookies while warm.

CARAMEL ICING:

½ Cup Brown Sugar
1 Cup Powdered Sugar
4 Tbsp. Milk
¼ tsp. vanilla
3 Tbsp. Butter

Combine brown sugar, butter, milk and vanilla in a medium saucepan and bring to a rolling boil. Remove from heat and stir until cool; add powdered sugar and frost cookies.

DOUBLE CHOCOLATE BROWNIES

1/2 Cup Crisco
16 oz. Chocolate Syrup
1 Cup Sugar
1 ¼ Cup Flour
4 Eggs
½ Tsp. Salt
1 Tsp. Vanilla
1 Cup Chopped Nuts

Blend Crisco and sugar together. Add eggs and beat until well mixed. Add vanilla, chocolate syrup, flour and salt. When mixed, pour into a greased and floured 13x9 pan; bake at 350 degrees for 30-35 minutes. Top with Quick Frosting:

QUICK FROSTING FOR BROWNIES

2/3 Cup Sugar
¼ Tsp. Salt
3 Tbsp. Milk
½ Cup Chocolate Chips
2 Tbsp. Crisco

Combine sugar, milk, Crisco and salt. Bring to a boil and boil for 30 seconds. Remove from heat and stir in chocolate chips until melted. Cool 10 minutes and spread on brownies.

CHERRY BARS

1 White Cake Mix
1 Can Cherry Pie Filling
6 Tbsp. Butter
2 Tbsp. Butter
1 Cup Oats
½ Cup Brown Sugar
1 Egg
¼ Cup Oats
Nuts (optional)
Coconut (optional)

Mix the cake mix, 6 tablespoons butter and 1 cup rolled oats; add egg. Reserve 1 cup of the crumbs. Press remaining in 13x9 pan. Spread cherry pie filling on top. To the 1 cup crumbs, add 2 tablespoons butter, brown sugar, ¼ cup oats, nuts and coconut. Put on top of cherry pie filling and bake at 350 degrees for 25 minutes.

CARAMEL APPLE WALNUT SQUARES

1 ¾ Cups Flour
1 Cup Quick Oats
½ Cup Brown Sugar
½ Tsp. Salt
1 Cup Cold Butter
1 Cup Walnuts
20 Caramels Unwrapped
14 oz. Eagle Brand Milk
1 Can Apple Pie Filling

PREHEAT oven to 375 degrees. In large bowl, combine flour, oats, sugar, baking soda and salt; cut in butter until crumbly. Reserving 1 ½ cups crumb mixture, press remainder on bottom of 13x9 pan and bake for 15 minutes. Add walnuts to reserved crumb mixture. In heavy saucepan, over low heat, melt caramels with Eagle brand milk, stirring until smooth. Spoon apple filling over prepared crust; top with caramel mixture then reserved crumb mixture. Bake 20 minutes or until set. Cool. Serve warm with ice cream.

CHERRY CHEESE BROWNIE SQUARES

1 Family Size Brownie Mix
8 oz. Cream Cheese
1 Can Eagle Brand Milk
1 Egg
1 Tsp. Almond Extract
1 Can Cherry Pie Filling

PREHEAT oven to 350 degrees. Prepare brownie mix as directed; spread into a 9x13 pan; bake for 20 minutes. Meanwhile, in small mixer bowl, beat cheese until fluffy. Gradually beat in Eagle Brand Milk, then egg and ½ tsp. almond extract. Pour evenly over brownie layer; bake 25 minutes longer or until set; cool; Chill. Stir remaining ½ tsp. almond extract into cherry filling; spoon over brownie squares and serve.

ICEBOX COOKIES

1 Cup Butter
1 Tsp. Cream of Tartar
2 Cups Brown Sugar
4 Cups Flour
2 Eggs
¾ Tsp. Vanilla
1 Tsp. Baking Soda
1 Cup Chopped Pecans

Mix all ingredients in order given. Roll into a roll and put in the refrigerator to chill. Slice and cook as needed. Bake at 350 degrees for 10-12 minutes.

STREUSEL BLUEBERRY MUFFINS

¾ Cup Milk
1 Cup Blueberries
¼ Cup Oil
1 Large Egg
2 Cups Flour
1 Cup Sugar

½ Tsp. Salt

PREHEAT OVEN TO 400 degrees. Grease only the bottoms of 12 medium muffin cups, or line with paper baking cups. Beat milk, oil and egg in a large bowl with a fork or wire whisk. Stir in flour, sugar, baking powder and salt all at once, just until flour is moistened. (Batter will be lumpy). Fold in blueberries. Divide batter evenly in muffin pans. Sprinkle each with 1 Tbsp. of Streusel Topping and bake 20-25 minutes or until golden brown. If baked in greased pan, let stand about 5 minutes then remove to wire rack. If baked in paper cups, immediately remove from the pan to wire rack.

STREUSEL TOPPING

¼ Cup Flour
¼ Cup Brown Sugar
¼ Tsp. Cinnamon
2 Tbsp. Firm Butter

Mix flour, brown sugar and cinnamon in medium bowl. Cut in butter, using fork or pastry blender. Sprinkle on tops of muffins.

APPLESAUCE MUFFINS

1 ¼ Cup Applesauce
2 Tsp. Baking Powder
1 Egg
¾ Tsp. Baking Soda
2 Tbsp. Oil
1 Tsp. Cinnamon
¼ Cup Honey
½ Tsp. Nutmeg
1 Cup Wheat Flour
1/3 Cup Raisins
1 Cup Flour

In a large bowl, beat together applesauce, egg, oil and honey. Sift in flours, baking powder, baking soda, cinnamon and nutmeg; stirring just to moisten. Stir in raisins and divide batter among 12 muffin cups coated with nonstick cooking spray. Bake at 375 degrees for 20 minutes.

MACINTOSH APPLE MUFFINS

1 ¼ Cups Oil
1 Tsp. Cinnamon
2 Cups Sugar
1 Tsp. Salt
3 Cups Flour
2 Cups Apples (Peeled & Chopped)
3 Eggs
2 Tsp. Vanilla
1 Cup Chopped Pecans
1 Tsp. Baking Soda
1 Cup Coconut

Mix all ingredients together until well-blended. Fill greased muffin tins about 2/3 full; Bake in 350 degree oven for 25 minutes or until golden brown. These muffins will not have much of a crown. They are very dense in texture. Makes 2-3 dozen

BANANA CRUMB MUFFINS

1 ½ Cups Flour
1/3 Cup Butter Melted
1 Tsp. Baking Soda
½ Tsp. Salt
3 Bananas Mashed
¾ Cup Sugar
1 Egg
1 Tsp. Baking Powder

TOPPING

1/3 Cup Brown Sugar
2 Tbsp. Flour
¼ Tsp. Cinnamon
1 Tbsp. Butter

PREHEAT oven to 375 degrees. Lightly grease 10 muffin cups or line with paper liners. In a large bowl, mix together flour, baking soda, baking powder and salt. In another bowl, beat together bananas, sugar, egg and melted butter. Stir the banana mixture into the flour mixture just until moistened. Spoon batter into prepared muffin tins. In a small bowl, mix together brown sugar, 2 Tbsp. Flour and cinnamon; cut in butter until mixture resembles coarse cornmeal. Sprinkle topping over muffins. Bake for 18-20 minutes or until toothpick inserted into center of muffin comes out clean.

COFFEE CAKE MUFFINS

1 ½ Cups Flour
¼ Cup Shortening
½ Cup Sugar
1 Egg Beaten
2 Tsp. Baking Powder
½ Cup Milk
½ Tsp. Salt
1 ½ Tsp. Cinnamon

TOPPING

½ Cup Brown Sugar
2 Tsp. Cinnamon
½ Cup Chopped Apples
2 Tbsp. Butter Melted
2 Tbsp. Flour

Sift dry ingredients into bowl. Cut in shortening until mixture resembles coarse crumbs. Blend in egg and milk and stir until moistened. Fill greased and floured tins 2/3 full. Combine brown sugar, chopped apples, flour, cinnamon and melted butter for topping and sprinkle on top of muffins. Bake at 375 degrees for 20 minutes. Makes 12

FRIENDSHIP TEA MUFFINS

1 Stick Butter
½ Tsp. Baking Soda
¾ Cup Brown Sugar
1 Cup Buttermilk
¼ Cup Sugar
½ Cup Walnuts
2 Eggs
¾ Cup Mini Chocolate Chips
1 ¾ Cups Flour
1/3 Cup White Chocolate Chips
2 Tsp. Baking Powder

PREHEAT oven to 375 degrees. Blend butter and sugars until smooth. Add eggs and continue to mix until blended. In small bowl, mix flour baking powder and soda. Stir half of flour mixture into butter mixture; stir in buttermilk, then add remaining flour mixture. Fold in nuts and chips, being careful not to over mix. Spoon batter into greased muffin and bake for 20 minutes or until muffins are slightly golden brown.

SOUR CREAM BLUEBERRY MUFFINS

4 Eggs
1 Tsp. Salt
2 Cups Sugar
1 Tsp. Baking Soda
1 Cup Vegetable Oil
2 Tsp. Baking Powder
1 Tsp. Vanilla
2 Cups Sour Cream
4 Cups Flour
2-4 Cups Blueberries

Beat eggs, add sugar and beat again. Pour in oil. Add vanilla. Mix all together. Mix the dry ingredients together. Add alternately with sour cream to the first mixture. Gently fold in blueberries. Bake in 24 greased muffin tins at 400 degrees for 20 minutes.

OUTRAGEOUS BLUEBERRY MUFFINS

2 ¼ Cups Cake Flour
1 Tsp. Salt
1 ½ Cups Sugar
1 Tsp. Vanilla
¾ Cup Shortening
½ Tsp. Water
¾ Cup Milk
16 oz. Blueberries (if frozen, drain and dry)
2 Eggs
2 ½ Tsp. Baking Powder

PREHEAT oven to 350 degrees; Grease and flour muffin tins or line with paper liners. In large mixing bowl, combine flour, sugar, shortening, milk, eggs, baking powder, salt, vanilla and water. Blend at low speed for 2 minutes. Scrape sides of bowl and mix at high speed for 6 minutes. Fill muffin tins half full. Add 6-10 blueberries to each cup, mixing in several and leaving some on top. Bake for 25 minutes. Remove from oven and let cool in pan for 10 minutes. Turn out and allow to cool completely. Makes 24 muffins

-NOTES-

CAKES AND DESSERTS

OATMEAL CAKE

1 Cup Oats
1 Cup Sugar
1 ½ Cups Boiling Water
1 Cup Brown Sugar
½ Cup Butter
2 Eggs
1 ½ Cups Flour
1 Tsp. Baking Soda
½ Tsp. Salt
½ Tsp. Cinnamon
1 Tsp. Vanilla

PREHEAT oven to 350 degrees. In large bowl mix oats, water and butter and let stand for about 5 minutes; add remainder of ingredients and pour into a 9x13 pan and bake for 30 minutes.

TOPPING

1 Cup Coconut
7 Tbsp. Butter
1 Cup Brown Sugar
½ cup milk
1 tsp. vanilla

Mix all ingredients until well blended; spread over warm cake and broil on low until bubbly and light brown.

FRESH APPLE CAKE

2 cups sugar
1 ½ cups oil
1 tsp. cinnamon
2 eggs
3 cups flour
1 tsp. nutmeg
1 tsp. baking soda
3 cups chopped apples
1 tsp. salt
1 cup chopped nuts

In a large bowl mix sugar and oil until well blended; add remainder of ingredients in order given and mix well; (batter will be thick). Spoon into a well-greased and floured Bundt pan and bake for 1 hour and ten minutes at 350 degrees I drizzle with powdered sugar glaze while warm, but can use caramel instead.

CARAMEL ICING FOR APPLE CAKE

1 Stick Butter
1 Cup Brown Sugar
2 Tbsp. Milk
1 ½ - 2 Cups Powdered Sugar

In medium saucepan combine butter, brown sugar and milk; cook over low heat until melted, remove from heat and add powdered sugar; beat until smooth. Spread on warm cake.

ICE CREAM CAKE

1 Pkg. Oreos Crushed
2 Tbsp. Butter Melted
1 8 oz. Jar Caramel Topping
1 8 oz. Jar Hot Fudge Sauce
8 oz. Whipping Cream
½ Cup Slivered Almonds
½ Gallon Ice Cream

Set Ice Cream of your choice out to soften. Crush Oreos in the food processor and mix with melted butter. Press into the bottom and up sides of a 9x13 pan. Heat hot fudge sauce and pour in the bottom of the crust. Spread ice cream over hot fudge, then you can drizzle more hot fudge sauce if you like. Whip the whipping cream as directed and put over the ice cream layer; drizzle with caramel sauce and sprinkle with almonds. You can add marshmallows, fruit or any kind of ice cream topping to this.

DELICIOUS CAKE

1 yellow cake mix
8 oz. sour cream
½ cup water
3 eggs
½ cup chopped nuts
1 sm. instant vanilla pudding
½ cup oil
16 oz. chocolate chips

4 oz. German Chocolate grated
Pecan Halves (for garnish)

In large bowl mix cake mix, sour cream, water, eggs, pudding and oil. Fold in nuts, chocolate and chocolate chips. Pour into greased and floured Bundt cake pan and bake 350 degrees for 1 hour. Sprinkle with powdered sugar while hot or melt the chocolate candy bars and pour over the top; garnish with pecan halves.

BANANA SPLIT CAKE

2 Cups Graham Cracker Crumbs
1 Cup Butter
1 Box Powdered Sugar
2 Eggs
4-5 Large Bananas
2 Cans Crushed Pineapple
1 Large Tub Cool Whip
½ Cup Chopped Nuts
1 Jar Maraschino Cherries

Melt ½ cup butter and mix with graham cracker crumbs and ½ cup powdered sugar; press onto bottom of 9x13 pan. Beat eggs, ½ cup melted butter and powdered sugar about 10 minutes then spread over crust. Layer bananas and pineapple; top with cool whip, sprinkle with nuts and garnish with maraschino cherries. Keep refrigerated.

HONEY BUN CAKE

1 Yellow Cake Mix
2/3 Cup Oil
4 Eggs
8 oz. Sour Cream
1 Cup Brown Sugar
1/3 Cup Chopped Pecans
2 Tsp. ground cinnamon
1 Cup Powdered Sugar
1 Tbsp. Milk
1 Tsp. Vanilla

PREHEAT oven to 350 degrees (325 for dark pans). Grease and lightly flour 13x9 inch pan. In large bowl beat dry cake mix, oil, eggs and sour cream with mixer on medium for 2 minutes. Spread half the batter in pan. Stir together brown sugar, pecans and cinnamon; sprinkle over batter in pan. Carefully spread remaining batter evenly over pecan mixture. Bake 44-48 minutes or until deep golden brown. Stir powdered sugar, milk and vanilla until thin enough to spread. Prick surface of warm cake several times with a fork. Spread powdered sugar mixture over cake. Cool completely

GOOEY PUMPKIN BUTTER CAKE

Cake:
1 Yellow Cake Mix
1 Egg
8 Tbsp. Butter (melted)

PREHEAT oven to 350 degrees. Combine all of the ingredients and mix well with mixer. Pat the mixture into the bottom of a lightly greased 13x9 pan. Prepare filling.

Filling:

8 oz. Cream Cheese
1 Can Pumpkin
3 Eggs
1 Tsp. Vanilla
8 Tbsp. Butter (melted)
1 Lb. Powdered Sugar
1 Tsp. Cinnamon
1 Tsp. Nutmeg

To make the filling: In a large bowl, beat the cream cheese and pumpkin until smooth. Add the eggs, vanilla, and butter and beat together. Next, add the powdered sugar, cinnamon, and nutmeg, mix well. Spread the pumpkin mixture over cake batter and bake for 40-50 minutes. Make sure not to over-bake as the center should be a little gooey.

VARIATIONS:

GOOEY PINEAPPLE CAKE: instead of the pumpkin add a drained 20 oz. can of crushed pineapple to the cream cheese filling.

GOOEY BANANA CAKE: Instead of pumpkin add 2 ripe bananas to the cream cheese filling.

GOOEY PEANUT BUTTER CAKE: Use a chocolate cake mix. Add 1 cup creamy peanut butter to the cream cheese filling instead of the pumpkin.

RUM CAKE

1 Yellow Cake Mix (butter)
4 eggs
1 Cup Water
1 Box Instant Vanilla Pudding
1 Tsp. Rum Flavoring
¼ Cup Oil

PREHEAT oven to 350 degrees. In mixing bowl combine, cake mix, eggs, water, rum flavoring, pudding and oil; beat until well blended. Pour into greased and floured Bundt cake pan and bake for 45 minutes to 1 hour. Poke holes in warm cake and pour syrup over:

SYRUP:

1 Cup Sugar
1/3 Cup Water
½ Cup Butter
1 Tsp. Rum Flavoring or
1 shot of Rum

Heat all but rum or flavoring until butter is melted. Remove from heat add in flavoring or rum and stir well. Pour over cake.

PUMPKIN SHEET CAKE

2 Cups Sugar
2 Tsp. Cinnamon
1 Cup Oil
1 Tsp. Baking Powder
2 Tsp. Baking Soda (Dissolved in water)
¾ Tsp. Salt
2 Cups Pumpkin
4 Eggs Beaten
2 Cups Flour

Mix together sugar, oil and soda; add eggs. Sift together dry ingredients and add to creamed mixture; beat well. Add pumpkin to batter and beat well. Spread in a 11x17 inch sheet cake pan and bake at 350 degrees for 20 minutes. Frost with Cream Cheese frosting and sprinkle with chopped nuts.

MARSHMALLOW CHERRY CAKE

1 Pkg. Large Marshmallows
1 Can Cherry Pie Filling
1 Pkg. Cherry Jell-O
1 Yellow Cake Mix
(May use Chocolate or White)

PREHEAT oven to 350 degrees. Grease and flour 13x9 pan; cover bottom with marshmallows; Mix cake mix as directed and pour over marshmallows; Mix Jell-O with pie filling and spoon over top of cake batter. Bake for 30-35 minutes. Cherries will go to the bottom and marshmallows will come to top, melt and form frosting!

FUDGE SHEET CAKE & FROSTING

2 Cups Sugar
1 Cup Water
2 Cups Flour
½ Cup Sour Milk
½ Tsp. Salt
2 Eggs Beaten
½ Cup Margarine
1 Tsp. Vanilla
½ Cup Crisco
1 Tsp. Baking Soda
4 Tbsp. Cocoa
1 Tsp. Cinnamon

Stir together sugar, flour and salt. Bring to a rapid boil the margarine, Crisco, cocoa and water. Remove mixture from heat; add the sugar and flour mixture and stir well; add remaining ingredients and beat until well blended. Pour into a 11x17 inch sheet cake pan and bake at 400 degrees for 20 minutes. Frost cake immediately after removing from oven.

FROSTING:

½ Cup Margarine
1 Tsp. Vanilla
4 Tbsp. Cocoa
1 Cup Chopped Nuts
1 Lb. Powdered Sugar
6 Tbsp. Milk

Combine margarine, cocoa and milk and bring to a boil; remove from heat and add remaining ingredients; Spread over hot cake.

SPICE CAKE

2 Eggs Beaten
½ Tsp. Cloves
1 Cup Sugar
½ Tsp. Ginger
1 Cup Sour Cream
½ Tsp. Cinnamon
½ Cup Butter Melted
1 ½ Cups Flour
1 Tsp. Baking Soda

Cream butter, sugar and sour cream; add eggs and mix well; Add dry ingredients and mix; pour into 9x13 pan and bake at 350 degrees for 30-35 minutes. Cool and frost with cream cheese or white frosting.

TWINKIE CAKE

1 Box Twinkies
3-4 Bananas Sliced
1 Can Crushed Pineapple
2 Boxes Instant Vanilla Pudding
1 Large Tub Cool Whip
½ -3/4 Cup Chopped Pecans

Drain pineapple; Split Twinkies in half long ways and place in 9x13; cover with pudding (prepared as directed on box); cover with pineapple; put bananas over pineapple; top with cool whip and sprinkle with pecans. Keep in refrigerator.

PUMPKIN DUMP CAKE

2 Cans Pumpkin
4 Eggs
1 ½ Cups Sugar
1 Can Evaporated Milk
2 ¾ Tsp. Pumpkin Pie Spice
1 Yellow Cake Mix
2 Sticks Butter
¾ Cup Chopped Pecans

Mix pumpkin, sugar, eggs, milk and pumpkin pie spice; pour into a 9x13 pan; Sprinkle dry yellow cake mix on top; Melt 2 sticks of butter and pour over cake mix: Sprinkle with pecans; Bake at 350 degrees for 1 hour.

MISSISSIPPI MUD CAKE

2 Sticks Butter
1 Tsp. Baking Powder
2 Cups Sugar
1 Tsp. Vanilla
2 Tbsp. Cocoa
1 ½ Cups Flour
4 Eggs
1 Cup Coconut
1 Large Jar Marshmallow Crème

Mix butter, sugar, cocoa, eggs, baking powder, vanilla and coconut; Pour on 11x15 sheet cake pan and bake at 350 degrees for 35-40 minutes. Spread with marshmallow crème while hot then frost with:

FROSTING:

1 Stick Butter
1 Lb. Powdered Sugar
½ Cup Cocoa
1 Tsp. Vanilla
½ Cup Milnot

Combine all ingredients and beat until fluffy; Ice cake when it is cool.

POUND CAKE

1 Cup Butter
½ Cup Shortening
3 Cups Flour
1 Cup Milk
5 Eggs
3 Cups Sugar
½ Tsp. Baking Powder
½ Tsp. Salt
1 Tsp. Vanilla
1 Tsp. Almond Extract
1 ½ Tsp. Butter Extract

PREHEAT oven to 325 degrees; grease and flour 2 loaf pans. Cream together butter, shortening and sugar. Combine flour, baking powder and salt. Add flour mixture to sugar mixture; alternate with flour mixture, egg, milk etc. until well blended; add extracts and stir well. Pour into loaf pans and bake for 1 ½ hours.

CAKE THAT DON'T LAST

3 Cups Flour
1 ½ Cups Oil
2 Cups Sugar
2 Cups Bananas Mashed
1 Tsp. Baking Soda
1 Can Crushed Pineapple
1 Tsp. Salt
1 Tsp. Cinnamon
1 ½ Tsp. Vanilla
1 Cup Nuts
3 Eggs

PREHEAT oven to 350 degrees. DO NOT DRAIN PINEAPPLE. Combine all ingredients in order given and stir until well blended. Pour into a 9x13 pan and bake for 1 hour and 20 minutes. When cool frost with Cream Cheese Icing.

FESTIVE EGGNOG CAKE

4 Large Eggs
½ Cup Oil
1 Yellow Cake Mix
2 Tsp. Rum Extract
1 Pkg. Instant Vanilla Pudding
1 Tsp. Nutmeg
½ Cup Water
10 oz. Holiday Morsels
16 oz. Cream Cheese Frosting

PREHEAT oven to 350 degrees; Grease and flour a 9x13 pan. Beat eggs in large mixer bowl for 1 minute or until frothy; add cake mix, water, oil, rum extract and nutmeg. Beat on medium speed for 2 minutes. Stir in ½ cup morsels. Spread in prepared pan. Sprinkle ½ cup morsels over batter. Bake for 35-40 minutes. Cool and spread with frosting; sprinkle with remaining 2/3 cup morsels.
May use French Vanilla Cake mix and French Vanilla Instant Pudding

ZUCCHINI PINEAPPLE CAKE

3 Eggs
2 Cups Sugar
1 Cup Oil
2 Cups Grated Zucchini
2 Tsp. Vanilla
3 Cups Flour
½ Tsp. Cinnamon
½ Tsp. Baking Powder
½ Tsp. Nutmeg
1 Tsp. Baking Soda
1 Cup Crushed Pineapple
1 Tsp. Salt
1 ½ Cup Nuts

Mix eggs, sugar and oil; beat until well blended; drain pineapple; add all the rest of the ingredients and stir until well mixed. Pour into a 9x13 pan and bake at 325 degrees for 1-1 ½ hours.

ICING:

8 oz. Cream Cheese
½ Cup Butter
1 Lb. Powdered Sugar
1 Tsp. Vanilla
½ Cup Drained Crushed Pineapple

Mix all ingredients until well blended and no lumps then spread on cooled cake.

ZUCCHINI CHOCOLATE CAKE

½ Cup Butter
1 Tsp. Vanilla
½ Cup Oil
2 Cups Zucchini (grated)
2 Eggs
1 ¾ Cups Sugar
½ Cup Sour Milk
2 ½ Cups Flour
½ Tsp. Cinnamon
½ Tsp. Baking Powder
½ Tsp. Cloves
1 Tsp. Baking Soda
4 Tbsp. Cocoa

Cream butter, oil and sugar; add eggs, vanilla, milk. Add dry ingredients stirring until well blended; stir in zucchini then pour into a 9x13 inch pan and bake at 325 degrees for 40-50 minutes. When cool frost with cream cheese icing.

CREAM CHEESE ICING:

8 oz. Cream Cheese
½ Cup Margarine or Butter
1 Lb. Powdered Sugar (or more)
1 Tsp. Vanilla
1 Tbsp. Milk

Beat all ingredients together until well blended and no lumps. Spread on cooled cake.

FRUIT COCKTAIL CAKE

2 Cups Sugar
2 Cups Flour
2 Eggs
½ Tsp. Baking Soda
16 oz. Fruit Cocktail

Mix all ingredients until well blended: Pour in a greased 9x13 pan and bake at 350 degrees for 25 minutes or until it test done. Ice while it is hot. Use Golden Broiled Topping.

GOLDEN BROILED TOPPING

½ Cup Melted Butter
1 ½ Cup Sugar
1 Cup Canned Cream
1 Cup Coconut
1 Cup Chopped Nuts

Bring butter, sugar and cream to a boil add coconut and nuts and bring back to a boil. Pour over hot cake.

APRICOT-COCONUT CAKE

1 Cup Coconut
¾ Cup Butter
3 Cups Flour
2 Tsp. Baking Powder
½ Tsp. Salt
1 ½ Cups Sugar
4 Large Eggs
1 Tsp. Vanilla
1 ¼ Cups Apricot Preserves
1 Cup Whole Milk
1 Cup Heavy Cream
¼ Cup Sour Cream
2 Tbsp. Powdered Sugar

PREHEAT oven to 350. Toast the coconut on a baking sheet, tossing occasionally, until golden, 10 to 12 minutes. Grease and flour two 8 inch round cake pans. In a large bowl, whisk together the flour, baking powder and salt. Using an electric mixer, beat the butter and sugar until fluffy. Beat in the eggs one at a time, then the vanilla and ¾ cup of the preserves. Alternately add the flour mixture and the milk, mixing just until incorporated. Divide the batter between the pans and bake 40-45 minutes or until it test done. Remove the cakes from the pans and let cool completely on wire racks. Beat cream, sour cream and powdered sugar until stiff peaks form. Spread ½ cup preserves on top of one of the cakes, place the other cake on top; frost with cream cheese mixture and press coconut on sides.

MOUNDS CAKE

1 Chocolate Cake Mix
1 Cup Coconut
1 Cup Milk
1 Pkg. Marshmallows
1 Cup Sugar
1 Cup Chocolate Chips

Mix and bake cake mix as directed on package. Combine coconut, marshmallows and ½ cup milk in large saucepan and heat until melted. Spread over cake. Combine ½ cup milk and sugar; heat until like syrup then add chocolate chips and stir until melted. Pour over marshmallow layer.

CARROT CAKE

2 Cups Sugar
1 ½ Cups Oil
2 Cups Flour
4 Eggs
2 Tsp. Baking Soda
3 Cups Grated Carrots
2 Tsp. Cinnamon (heaping)
1 Cup Chopped Nuts

Sift dry ingredients. Add Oil and eggs; beat. Add carrots and nuts. Bake in three 9-inch pans at 350 degrees for 30 minutes: Frost with cream cheese frosting when cool.

CREAM CHEESE FROSTING

8 oz. Cream Cheese
1 Box Powdered Sugar
1 Stick Oleo
1 Tsp. Vanilla
1 Cup Chopped Pecans

Mix together until smooth and spread between layers, on top and sides of cake.

RED VELVET CAKE

½ Cup Shortening
3 Tbsp. Cocoa
1 ½ Cups Sugar

2 ½ Cups Flour
2 Eggs
1 Cup Buttermilk
2 Tsp. Vanilla
1 Tsp. Salt
1 Tsp. Butter Flavoring
1Tbsp. Vinegar
1 ½ oz. Red Food Coloring
1 Tsp. Baking Soda

PREHEAT oven to 350 degrees. Cream Shortening, sugar, eggs and flavoring well. Make a paste of cocoa and food coloring and add to first mixture. Add flour and buttermilk, alternating, starting and ending with flour. Mix baking soda and vinegar and add to batter, blend. Bake for 20 -25 minutes in three 9 inch pans or two 10 inch pans.

FROSTING:

3 Tbsp. Flour
1 Cup Sugar
½ Tsp. Salt
2 Tsp. Vanilla
1 Cup Milk
¼ Tsp. Butter Flavoring
1 C. Shortening

Cook milk, flour and salt, stirring constantly on low heat. Let cool Cream shortening and sugar; add flavorings. Combine with first mixture and beat well.

ICE CREAM SANDWICH DESSERT

17 Small Ice Cream Sandwiches
¼ Cup Chocolate Syrup
12 oz. Caramel Topping
1 Chocolate Candy Bar Shaved
1 Tub Cool Whip

In 13x9 pan arrange sandwiches. Spread on caramel then cool whip. Drizzle with syrup; Sprinkle with candy bar. Cover and freeze at least 1 hour before serving.

ITALIAN CREAM CAKE

1 Cup Buttermilk
1 Cup Nuts
1 Tsp. Baking Powder
1 Cup Coconut
1 Stick Butter
½ Cup Shortening
2 Cups Sugar
1 Tsp. Vanilla
5 Eggs (separated)
2 Cups Flour

PREHEAT oven to 350 degrees. Mix buttermilk and baking soda; set aside. Blend margarine, shortening and sugar. Beat in egg yolks and vanilla. Alternately add flour and buttermilk. Beat egg whites, fold onto flour mixture then add nuts and coconut. Pour into round cake pans and bake for 25 minutes.

FROSTING:

1 Box Powdered Sugar
8 oz. Cream Cheese
1 Tsp. Vanilla
1 Stick Butter½ Cup Coconut

Combine sugar, vanilla, cream cheese and butter until well blended. Frost cake and sprinkle top with coconut.

APPLESAUCE CAKE

½ Cup Butter
½ Tsp. Nutmeg
1 Cup Brown Sugar
1 Tsp. Baking Soda
2 Eggs
¾ Cup Raisins
2 Cups Flour
1 Cup Chopped Nuts
½ Tsp. Salt
1 Cup Applesauce
1 Tsp. Cinnamon
½ Tsp. Cloves

Cream shortening and sugar until well blended. Add beaten eggs and blend well. Sift all dry ingredients together to which you add nuts and raisins. Add flour mixture and applesauce to egg mixture, stirring thoroughly. Bake at 350 degrees for 45-50 minutes in 9x13 pan

SAUCE FOR APPLESAUCE CAKE

3 Tbsp. Flour
1 ½ Cups Water
¾ Cup Sugar
2 Tbsp. Lemon Juice
2 Tbsp. Butter
1 Tsp. Vanilla

Melt butter in a saucepan. Add and blend thoroughly the flour, sugar and water. Cook until sauce thickens, stirring constantly. Remove from heat and add flavorings. Pour over cake.

TRIPLE LAYER CHOCOLATE CAKE

1 ¼ Cups Cocoa
1 Cup Boiling Water
1 ½ Cups Buttermilk
2 ¼ Cups Flour
2 Tsp. Baking Soda
1 Tsp. Baking Powder
½ Tsp. Salt
½ Cup Butter
2 ½ Cups Sugar
4 Eggs
1 Tsp. Vanilla

PREHEAT oven to 350 degrees. Grease and flour three 9 inch round cake pans. In bowl whisk boiling water and cocoa until smooth; stir in buttermilk. Reserve. In separate bowl, stir together flour, soda, baking powder and salt. In separate bowl on medium high speed, beat butter with sugar until light and fluffy. On low, beat in eggs and vanilla. Alternately beat in flour and cocoa mixtures. Divide batter among pans and bake 20-25 minutes. Cool on racks.

BUTTERCREAM FROSTING:

6 Cups Powdered Sugar
1 1/3 Cups Cocoa
1 Cup Butter
2/3 Cup Milk
2 Tsp. Vanilla
¼ Cup Corn Syrup

Combine sugar and cocoa. On medium high speed, beat butter until fluffy. On low gradually beat in sugar mixture until blended. Beat in milk and vanilla until smooth; beat in corn syrup until shiny. Place one layer of cake on serving plate; spread with frosting; repeat layering with remaining cake layers and frosting. Spread cake top and sides with remaining frosting.

HAWAIIAN CAKE

1 Yellow Cake Mix
½ Tsp. Vanilla
3 Eggs
1 Can Mandarin Oranges
2/3 Cup Oil (plus water to make ¾ Cup
1 Can Crushed Pineapple)
1 Pkg. Instant Coconut Pudding

DO NOT DRAIN ORANGES OR PINEAPPLE. Combine cake mix, eggs, oil, water mixture and oranges with juice; beat until well blended. Pour into sheet cake pan and bake at 350 degrees for 15-20 minutes. Cool completely. Fold together the pineapple, pudding, vanilla and cool whip until creamy. Spread over top of cake. Keep in refrigerator.

ONE EGG CAKE

1 Cup Milk
¼ Tsp. Salt
1 Cup Sugar
1 Cup Flour
1 Egg
1 Tsp. Baking Powder
1 Tsp. Vanilla
¼ Cup Shortening

Combine cream, sugar, egg and vanilla. Beat. Sift together the salt, flour and baking powder. Add to the first mixture. Bake 25-30 minutes at 350 degrees for 9x13 pan or 20 minutes for cupcakes. This is a good cake to use for shortcake. To make shortcake; split cake in half - length wise; put half on platter top with mashed, sweetened blackberries, strawberries or blueberries. Top with other half of cake and more fruit. Cover with cool whip and serve.

ICE WATER WHITE CAKE

½ Cup Shortening
½ Tsp. Salt
2 Cups Sugar
1 ½ Cups Ice Water
3 ½ Cups Flour
4 Eggs
4 Tsp. Baking Powder
1 Tsp. Vanilla

Beat egg whites until stiff; Cream sugar and shortening together. Add flour, baking powder, salt and ice water. Mix well. Fold in egg whites and vanilla. Pour in 9x13 pan and bake in 350 degree oven for 30-35 minutes or until center is done.

HOT MILK CAKE

2 Eggs
1 Tbsp. Butter
1 Cup Sugar
1 Tsp. Vanilla
1 Cup Flour
2 Tsp. Baking Powder
½ Cup Milk
Few Drops Almond Extract

Scald milk with butter. Beat eggs until foamy; add sugar and continue beating. Add part of flour that has been sifted with baking powder, then alternate hot milk and remaining flour. Add vanilla and almond extract. Pour into floured, 9x13 pan and bake at 325 degrees for 30 minutes or until top springs back when touched lightly. Dust top with powdered sugar while hot.

APPLE CAKE

2 Cups Flour
1 Can Apple Pie Filling
1 ½ Cups Sugar
2 Eggs
½ Tsp. Salt
¾ Cup Oil
1 Tsp. Cinnamon
½ Cup Nuts
1 Tsp. Baking Soda

Mix all ingredients in order given. Bake in ungreased 9x13 pan at 350 degrees for 35-45 minutes.

3-LAYER DESSERT

FIRST LAYER:
1 Cup Flour
½ Cup Pecans
2 Tbsp. Powdered Sugar
½ Cup Melted Butter

Mix all ingredients and press in bottom of 9x13 in pan. Bake at 350 degrees for 15 minutes. Cool.

SECOND LAYER:

8 oz. Cream Cheese
1 Cup Powdered Sugar
1 ½ Cup Cool Whip

Mix all ingredients until well blended and no lumps then spread on first layer.

THIRD LAYER:

3 Cups Milk
1 Pkg. Instant Vanilla Pudding
1 Pkg. Instant Chocolate Pudding
(MAY USE 2 BOXES OF LEMON PUDDING INSTEAD OF CHOCOLATE AND VANILLA)

Mix milk and puddings with a mixer; spread on top of second layer and top with cool whip. Can sprinkle finely chopped nuts over the top.

PINA COLADA BARS

1 Cup Butter
3 ½ Cups Sugar
2 ½ Cups Flour
¼ Tsp. Salt
8 Eggs
12 oz. Pineapple Juice
½ Cup Lemon Juice
1 Tsp. Lemon Zest
6 Tbsp. Cornstarch
1 Tsp. Baking Powder
½ Cup Coconut

PREHEAT oven to 325 degrees. On medium speed, beat butter and ½ Cup Sugar until smooth. On low speed, gradually beat in flour and salt until dough comes together. Press into bottom and 1 inch up on sides of sheet cake pan; prick with a fork. Bake 20 minutes or until golden brown. Meanwhile whisk together eggs, juices, zest and remaining 2 ½ cups sugar until blended. Whisk in cornstarch and baking powder until blended. Pour into crust and bake 25 minutes or until filling is set, sprinkle on coconut the last 5 minutes of baking time. Cool and serve.

LOWFAT ORANGE GLAZED COOKIE BARS

1 Cup Flour
½ Tsp. Baking Powder
¼ Tsp. Salt
3 Tbsp. Butter
1 ¼ Cups Powdered Sugar
1 Egg White
3 Tbsp. Orange Zest
1/3 Cup Low-Fat Milk

PREHEAT OVEN to 350 degrees. Grease cookie sheets. Combine flour, baking powder and salt. On medium speed, beat butter and ½ cup sugar until smooth. Add egg white and 2 tsp. zest; beat until blended. On low, alternately beat in flour mixture and milk. Drop by tablespoon onto baking sheets, flatten to 2 ½ inches round and bake for 7-8 minutes. Cool 5 minutes on baking sheet then put on cooling racks and cool completely. Stir remaining ¾ Cup sugar and 1 tsp. zest with 5 tsp. water. Spread over cookies and let stand until dry; 15-20 minutes. Make in cookies or bars

PEANUT BUTTER CUP BARS

60 Miniature Peanut
2 ½ Cups Butter
Butter Cups
2 Tsp. Vanilla
2 Sugar Cookie Mix
2/3 Cup Peanut Butter
4 Cups Powdered Sugar

PREHEAT oven to 350 degrees. Coat 9x13 pan with cooking spray. Quarter 36 peanut butter cups. On medium speed, beat cookie mix, 1 Cup butter, eggs, 2 tbsp. peanut butter and 1 tsp. vanilla until smooth. Stir in quartered peanut butter cups. Spread in pan and bake for 30 minutes or until test done. Cool in pan. On medium, beat remaining butter and vanilla until fluffy; beat in remaining peanut butter, sugar and 1 tbsp. water until fluffy. Spread over bars. Halve remaining peanut butter cups and garnish top; cut into bars.

LOW FAT LEMON TRIFLE

½ Cup Orange
2 Tbsp. Lemon Juice
Marmalade (low-sugar)
2 ½ Cups 1% Milk
1 Tbsp. Lemon Zest
2 Cups Low Fat Cool Whip
1 Angel Food Cake
2 Pkgs. Instant Sugar Free
Lemon Pudding

Heat Marmalade until just melted; stir in lemon juice. In large bowl whisk pudding mixes with milk until smooth. Fold in zest, then whipped topping. Cut cake into 1 inch pieces and place ½ in large trifle bowl. Brush cake with half of marmalade, and then spoon over half of pudding mixture. Repeat with remaining cake, marmalade and pudding. Top with cool whip and garnish with lemon slices.

EARTHQUAKE CAKE

1 German Chocolate Cake Mix
1 Tsp. Vanilla
1 Stick Butter Softened
1 Cup Chopped Pecans
8 oz. Cream Cheese
1 Cup Coconut
1 Box Powdered Sugar

Spray a 9x13 in pan with cooking spray. Spread nuts and coconut on bottom of pan. Mix cake according to directions; pour over nuts and coconut. Mix together the cream cheese, powdered sugar, vanilla and butter. Drop by spoonful on the cake batter (do not spread) to the outer edges of the cake, so cake can bake and seal around the filling. Bake in 350 degree oven for 50 minutes. Turn out of pan upside down on cake plate. Nuts and coconut make the topping. (Cool slightly before turning out on plate)

STRAWBERRY DELIGHT

2 ½ Cups Graham Cracker Crumbs
2 Cups Boiling Water
½ Cup Sugar
2/3 Cup Butter Melted
8oz. Cream Cheese
20 oz. Frozen Strawberries
1 Tub Cool Whip
2 Pkg. Strawberry Jell-O
½ Cup Walnuts
2 Cups Powdered Sugar

First Step:
Mix graham cracker crumbs, sugar and butter. Press in a pan to form a crust.

Second Step:
Mix Jell-O, water and strawberries. Set aside to congeal slightly.

Third Step:
Combine cream cheese, whipped topping, walnuts and powdered sugar. Pour into crumb crust. After

strawberry mixture has thickened pour over cream cheese layer.

BREAD PUDDING

2 Cups Bread (Cubed)
¾ Cup Sugar
4 Cups Milk (Scalded)
4 Eggs (Beaten)
2 Tbsp. Butter
1 Tsp. Vanilla
½ Tsp. Nutmeg
1 Tsp. Cinnamon
½ Cup Raisins

Soak bread in milk for 5 minutes. Add butter, salt and sugar. Pour over eggs; add remainder of ingredients and pour into greased baking dish. Bake over a pan of hot water in 350 degree oven until firm, about 45-50 minutes.

SAUCE:

½ Cup Sugar
¾ Cup water
Dash of Salt
½ Cup Orange Juice
1 Tbsp. Cornstarch
2 Tbsp. Lemon Juice
1 Tbsp. Butter

Mix all ingredients in saucepan over low heat until it comes to a boil. Remove from heat and pour over pudding.

GERMAN CHOCOLATE CAKE

½ Cup Boiling Water
1 Tsp. Vanilla
4 oz. Sweet Cooking
1 Tsp. Baking Soda
Chocolate
2 ½ Cups Four
1 Cup Butter
½ Tsp. Salt
2 Cups Sugar
1 Cup Buttermilk

4 Eggs
4 Eggs Whites Stiffly Beaten

PREHEAT oven to 350 degrees. Pour boiling water over chocolate, stir until chocolate is melted and set aside to cool. Cream butter and sugar until light and fluffy; add egg yolks one at a time. On low speed blend in chocolate and vanilla. Mix in flour, soda and salt alternately with buttermilk, beating after each addition until batter is smooth. Fold in egg whites. Divide batter into 2 or 3 layer pans which have been greased and floured (or lined with wax paper). Bake 30-35 minutes or until top springs back when lightly touched. Cool completely; fill layers and frost top with Coconut-Pecan Frosting.

COCONUT-PECAN FROSTING

1 Cup Evaporated Milk
1 Tsp. Vanilla
1 Cup Sugar
1 1/3 Cup Coconut
3 Egg Yolks
1 Cup Chopped Pecans
½ Cup Butter

Combine milk, sugar, egg yolks, butter and vanilla in small saucepan. Cook and stir over medium heat until thick, about 12 minutes. Stir in coconut and pecans. Beat until thick enough to spread.

DUMP CAKE

12 oz. Crushed Pineapple
½ Cup Butter
1 Can Cherry Pie Filling
1 Cup Pecans
1 Yellow or Lemon Cake Mix

Grease bottom of 9x13 pan. Drain Pineapple and dump into dish, dump in cherry pie filling and then dump dry cake mix on top of cherries. Try to spread all ingredients evenly as you dump them. Dot top of cake mix with butter, then sprinkle nuts on top. Bake at 325 degrees for 55-60 minutes or until brown.

CARROT CAKE

2 Cups Sugar
1 Tsp. Salt
2 Cups Flour
1 Tsp. Cinnamon
1 Tsp. Baking Soda
1 Tsp. Allspice
1 ½ Cups Oil
4 Eggs
3 Cups Grated Carrots
1 Cup Chopped Nuts

PREHEAT oven to 350 degrees. Grease and flour 9x13 pan or two 9 inch layer pans; Combine the sugar, flour, salt, cinnamon, soda and oil. With mixer beat inn the eggs one at a time. Stir in the carrots. Pour the batter into the prepared pan and bake for 50 minutes; less time if using 9 inch pans. Cool and frost with cream cheese icing.

CREAM CHEESE FROSTING

¾ Cup Butter
8 oz. Cream Cheese
1 Tsp. Vanilla
3 Cups Powdered Sugar

In a mixing bowl, beat butter, cream cheese and vanilla until smooth. Gradually beat in powdered sugar until well blended and desired consistency. Spread on cooled cake.

BUTTERCREAM FROSTING

½ Cup Shortening
½ Cup Butter
1 Tsp. Vanilla
4 Cups Powdered Sugar
3 Tbsp. Milk

In a mixing bowl, cream shortening and butter; add vanilla. Gradually beat in sugar. Add milk; beat until light and fluffy. Frost a two-layer or 9x13 cake.

SEVEN MINUTE FROSTING

1 ¾ Cups Sugar
½ Cup Water
4 Egg Whites Room Temperature
½ Tsp. Cream of Tartar
1 Tsp. Vanilla

In a saucepan, bring sugar and water to a boil. Boil for 3-4 minutes or until a candy thermometer reads 242 degrees. Meanwhile, beat egg whites and cream of tartar in a mixing bowl until foamy. Slowly pour in hot sugar mixture; continue to beat on high for 7 minutes or until stiff peaks form. Add vanilla. Continue beating until frosting reaches desired consistency, about 2 minutes.

CHOCOLATE SOUR CREAM FROSTING

½ Cup Butter
3 oz. Unsweetened Chocolate
3 oz. Semisweet Chocolate
5 Cups Powdered Sugar
1 Cup Sour Cream
2 Tsp. Vanilla

In a medium saucepan, melt butter and chocolate over low heat. Cool 5 minutes. In a mixing bowl, combine sugar, sour cream and vanilla. Add chocolate mixture and beat until smooth. This will frost a 3 layer cake. This is good on chocolate, white or yellow cake.

MOCHA FROSTING

1 ½ Cups Powdered Sugar
½ Cup Cocoa
2 Tsp. Instant Coffee Crystals
Pinch of Salt
3 Cups Whipping Cream

Combine sugar, cocoa, coffee and salt in a mixing bowl. Stir in cream; cover and chill with beater for 30 minutes. Beat frosting until stiff peaks form.

COFFEE CAKE

2 Cups Sugar

1 Cup Chopped Nuts
2 Tbsp. Cinnamon
½ Cup Butter
2 Eggs
1 Tbsp. Vanilla
1 Tbsp. Lemon Juice
2 Cups Flour
½ Tsp. Baking Powder
1 Tsp. Salt
½ Pint Sour Cream
1 Tsp. Baking Soda

PREHEAT oven to 350 degrees. Mix and set aside 1 cup of sugar, the nuts and cinnamon. Cream the butter; beat in remaining sugar and the eggs. Add vanilla and lemon juice. Sift the dry ingredients together and add alternately to the butter mixture with sour cream. Pour half of the batter into a buttered 9x9 pan; sprinkle with ½ the cinnamon mixture. Spread on remaining batter and top with rest of the cinnamon mixture. Bake for 35 minutes.

STREUSEL COFFEE CAKE

1 Cup Sugar
1 Tsp. Baking Powder
3 Tbsp. Melted Butter
1 Cup Brown Sugar
1 Egg
4 Tbsp. Melted Butter
¾ Cup Milk
2 Tbsp. Flour
1 ½ Cups Flour
4 Tsp. Cinnamon

Mix sugar, 3 tbsp. butter, egg, milk, flour, baking powder and beat well. For topping mix brown sugar, 4 tbsp. butter, 2 tbsp. flour and cinnamon and set aside. Pour1/2 of batter into greased 8x8 pan (or loaf pan) sprinkle with ¼ of the topping and pour rest of batter on top then rest of topping. Bake at350 degrees for 30 minutes or until test done.

HAWAIIAN COFFEE CAKE-SUGAR FREE

2 Large Eggs
1 Cup Crushed Pineapple

2/3 Cup Pineapple Juice (drained)
¼ Cup Butter
1 Cup Coconut
2 Cup Flour
½ Tsp. Baking Soda
2 Tsp. Baking Powder
2 Tsp. Cinnamon

TOPPING

In a mixing bowl, beat together eggs, pineapple juice and butter. Add flour, baking soda and baking powder, beat well. Stir in the pineapple and coconut. Spoon into greased and floured 9 inch round pan. Spread batter evenly. For topping toss cinnamon and 1 cup crushed pineapple together and sprinkle over batter. Bake at 350 degrees for 20 to 25 minutes or until firm to the touch.

PUMPKIN ROLL

Set out 8 oz. Cream Cheese to get room temperature
3 Eggs
2/3 Cup Pumpkin
1 Cup Sugar
½ Tsp. Cinnamon
¾ Cup Flour
1 Tsp. Baking Powder
½ Cup Chopped Nuts (optional)

Mix all ingredients except nuts. Line a sheet cake pan with wax paper. Pour in mixture and spread evenly. Sprinkle on nuts and bake 10-15 minutes at 375 degrees. Turn upside down on kitchen towel that is covered with powdered sugar, remove wax paper and roll up in towel. Cool 20 minutes. Unroll and spread with filling. Reroll and wrap in foil. Refrigerate 1 ½ hours before serving.

FILLING

8 oz. Cream Cheese
2 Tbsp. Butter
¾ Tsp. Vanilla
1 Cup Powdered Sugar

Mix all ingredients until a creamy consistency with no lumps then spread on pumpkin roll and roll up and wrap in foil. Store in refrigerator; slice and serve.

LEMON BARS

1 Cup Butter
4 Eggs
½ Cup Powdered Sugar
2 Cups Sugar
2 Cups Flour
4 Tbsp. Flour
¼ Tsp. Salt
4 Tbsp. Lemon Juice
2 Tsp. Lemon Zest

Crust: blend butter, powdered sugar, flour and salt by hand and press into sheet cake pan. Bake at 325 degrees for 20 minutes. While crust is baking, mix eggs, sugar, 4 tbsp. flour and lemon juice. Pour over baked crust, return to oven and bake for 25 minutes. Remove from oven and sprinkle with powdered sugar. May add ¼ cup finely chopped nuts to crust if desired.

PEANUT BUTTER BROWNIE TRIFLE

1 Brownie Mix (9x13)
2 Pkg. Vanilla Pudding (Instant)
10 oz. Peanut Butter Chips
1 Cup Creamy Peanut Butter
26 oz. Mini Peanut Butter Cups
4 Tsp. Vanilla
4 Cups Cold Milk
24 oz. Cool Whip

Prepare brownie mix as directed. Stir in peanut butter chips. Bake at 350 degrees for 20-25 minutes. Cool. Cut into ¾ inch pieces. Cut peanut butter cups in half. Set aside 1/3 for garnish. In large bowl whisk milk and pudding mixes for 2 minutes or until soft-set. Add peanut butter and vanilla and mix well. Fold in ½ of cool whip. Place 1/3 of brownies in a 5 quart glass bowl; top with 1/3 of remaining peanut butter cups. Spoon a third of budding mixture over top. Repeat layers twice. Cover with remaining cool whip and garnish with reserved peanut butter cups. Refrigerate until chilled.

DIRT

1 Pkg. Oreo Cookies
1 Cup Powdered Sugar
1 Large Tub Cool Whip
2 Pkg. French Vanilla Pudding (Instant)
8oz. Cream Cheese
3 Cups Milk
¼ Cup Butter

Crumble 2/3 package of Oreo's in 13x9 pan. In bowl mix cool whip, cream cheese, butter and powdered sugar. In large bowl mix pudding and milk; stir in cream cheese mixture and pour over cookies. Crumble remaining cookies on top. Refrigerate.

BLACK FOREST CHOCOLATE CHEESECAKE

1 ½ Cups Oreo Crumbs
3 Tbsp. Melted Butter
16 oz. Cream Cheese
3 Eggs
14 oz. Chocolate Sweetened
3 Tbsp. Cornstarch
Condensed Milk
1 Tsp. Almond Extract

PREHEAT oven to 300 degrees. Combine crumbs and butter; press firmly on bottom of 9 inch spring-form pan. In large bowl, beat cheese until fluffy. Gradually beat in milk until smooth. Add eggs, cornstarch and almond extract; mix well. Pour into pan and bake 55 minutes or until center is set. Cool. Chill. Top with cherry pie filling before serving.

COFFEE CAKE ROLLS

¾ Cup Sugar
1 Cup Shortening
¾ Cup Water
2 Eggs Beaten
½ Tsp. Salt
1 Cup Milk
1 Pkg. Yeast
6 Cups or more Flour

Mix together like bread. Let stand in a covered bowl until morning. Make into 4 balls, roll each like pie dough. Sprinkle with brown sugar, cinnamon, melted butter and nuts. Roll up and let stand for 1 hour then bake on cookie sheet at 350 degrees for 30 minutes or until brown.

FRUIT PIZZA

½ Cup Butter
½ Cup Shortening
½ Cup Sugar
2 Eggs
2 ¾ Cups Flour
1 Tsp. Baking Soda
1 Tsp. Salt
2 Tsp. Cream of Tartar
16 oz. Cream Cheese
¼ Cup Sugar
2 Tbsp. Fruit Juice
1 Can Peaches Drained
1 Can Pineapple Drained
3-4 Bananas
1 Pint Strawberries
2 Kiwi

Make crust by creaming together butter, shortening and ½ cup sugar; add eggs, flour, soda, salt and cream of tartar, mixing well. Bake at 350 degrees until light brown like a cookie. Cool. Mix together cream cheese, sugar and fruit juice; Spread on top of cooled crust. Add fruit on top. Chill until ready to serve.

CHOCOLATE HAZELNUT CREAM CAKE ROLL

½ Cup Flour
¼ Cup + 1 Tbsp. Cocoa
¼ Tsp. Baking Powder
¼ Tsp. Baking Soda
Pinch of Salt
4 Eggs Separated (divided)
¾ Cup Sugar
¼ Cup Water
1 Tsp. Vanilla

FILLING
12 Oz. Cool Whip
¼ Cup Hazelnut Liquor
½ Cup Chopped Hazelnuts

ICING

4 Oz. Semi-Sweet Chocolate
2 Tbsp. Butter
1 Tsp. Vanilla
3 Tbsp. Cool Whip

Sift dry ingredients together. Beat egg whites to soft peaks gradually add ½ cup sugar. Beat until stiff but not dry. Beat egg yolks, ¼ cup sugar, water, vanilla until thick (6 minutes). On low speed add dry ingredients to egg yolk mixture, and then fold in egg whites. Grease a sheet cake pan and line with buttered wax paper. Spread batter on wax paper and bake in 350 degree oven for 12-15 minutes. When done invert on towel sprinkled with powdered sugar; roll up from long side and cool.

Place cool whip in medium bowl and fold in liquor and nuts. Unroll cooled cake and spread with filling; re-roll.

Melt chocolate and butter; blend in vanilla and topping, ice cake roll and garnish with nuts.

-NOTES-

_____
_____
_____
_____
_____
_____
_____
_____
_____
_____
_____
_____
_____

BREADS – ROLLS - BISCUITS

BANANA BREAD

1 Cup Sugar
½ Cup Butter
1 Egg
1 Cup Mashed Bananas
3 Tbsp. Milk
½ Tsp. Baking Soda
2 Cups Flour
1 Tsp. Baking Powder
½ Cup Chopped Nuts

Mix sugar and butter together. Add eggs, banana, milk, soda, flour and baking powder; blend well and add nuts. Pour into greased and floured loaf pan and bake at 325 degrees for one hour.

PUMPKIN BREAD

1 Cup Oil
2 Tsp. Baking Soda
3 Cups Sugar
1 Tsp. Nutmeg
4 Eggs
2 Tsp. Cinnamon
2 Cups Pumpkin
½ Tsp. Allspice
3 1/3 Cups Flour
½ Cup Raisins
1 ½ Tsp. Salt
¾ Cup Nuts
½ Cup Chopped Dates
2/3 Cup Water

PREHEAT oven to 350 degrees; grease and flour 2 loaf pans. Cream oil and sugar; add eggs and pumpkin and beat for 5 minutes. Sift dry ingredients together; add the water to the dry ingredients. Combine the 2 mixtures ad fold in by hand the raisins and nuts. Fill pans half full of batter and bake for 1 hour and 15 minutes.

CRANBERRY ORANGE BREAD

2 Cups Flour
1 ½ Tsp. Baking Powder
1 Tsp. Ginger
½ Tsp. Baking Soda
½ Tsp. Salt
¼ Tsp. Nutmeg
1/3 Cup Butter
1 Cup Sugar
1 Tsp. Vanilla
2 Tsp. Grated Orange Peel
½ Cup Orange Juice
2 Eggs
1 Cup Chopped Cranberries
½ Cup Slivered Almonds

PREHEAT oven to 350 degrees. Mix flour, baking powder, ginger, soda, salt and nutmeg; set aside. Beat butter sugar and vanilla in large bowl on medium speed until light and fluffy. Add orange peel, orange juice and eggs; mix well. Gradually add to flour mixture, mixing just until moistened. Gently stir in cranberries and almonds. Divide batter evenly among 3 greased mini-loaf pans. Bake 35 minutes. Cool in pans 10 minutes. Remove from pans and cool completely on wire rack.

MOIST CRANBERRY BREAD

2 Cups Flour
1 ½ Tsp. Baking Powder
½ Tsp. Baking Soda
½ Tsp. Salt
1 Cup Sugar
1 Cup Chopped Cranberries
½ Cup Chopped Nuts
1 Beaten Egg
3 Tbsp. Vegetable Oil
1 Cup Orange Juice

PREHEAT oven to 350 degrees. Sift dry ingredients together in a bowl. Add cranberries and nuts, mixing to combine. In a small bowl add, egg, orange juice and oil whisking slightly together. Add to the dry mixture and mix just to combine. Pour into a greased loaf pan and bake for 1 hour or until test done.

APPLE BREAD

½ Cup Butter

1 Tsp. Baking Soda
1 Cup Sugar
1 Tsp. Cinnamon
1 Egg
½ Cup Cold Coffee
1 ½ Cups Flour
1 Cup Diced Apple
½ Tsp. Salt
½ Cup Chopped Nuts

Cream butter, sugar, and egg; add flour, salt, soda and cinnamon. Mix well. Add coffee and diced apple. Mix well and pour into greased loaf pan and bake at 350 degrees for 35-40 minutes.

ZUCCHINI BREAD

3 Eggs
1 Cup Oil
2 Cups Sugar
2 Cups Grated Zucchini
3 Cups Flour
3 Tsp. Vanilla
1 Tsp. Salt
1 Tsp. Baking Soda
¼ Tsp. Baking Powder
1 Tbsp. Cinnamon
½ Cup Chopped Nuts

In medium bowl mix sugar, oil and eggs until well blended. Add remaining ingredients and stir until mixed well. Pour into 2 well-greased and floured loaf pans. Bake at 325 degrees for 1 hour and 10 minutes.

YEAST ROLLS

2 Cups Milk (scalded)
½ Cup Sugar
1 Cup Shortening
1 Tsp. Salt
2 Eggs
6-8 Cups Flour
4 Pkg. Yeast
½ Cup Warm Water

Put yeast in a small bowl and add water; stir and let set. Mix sugar, shortening and eggs. Add ½ of the flour then pour in the yeast and mix well; stir in the milk and add enough flour to make medium dough that is not to stiff. Cover and let rise until double. Punch down and make into rolls or loafs and let rise again. Bake at 350 for 25-30 minutes.

OATMEAL YEAST ROLLS

1 Cup Oatmeal
1/3 Cup Warm Water
2 Cups Boiling Water
1 Tbsp. Sugar
2 Tbsp. Butter
6-7 Cups Flour
2/3 Cup Brown Sugar
2 Eggs
1 ½ Tsp. Salt
1 Cup Bran Cereal optional
2 Pkg. Yeast

Pour boiling water over oatmeal. Add Butter. Let cool. Mix yeast with water and 1 tbsp. sugar. Then add yeast, brown sugar, salt, and eggs. Mix well. Add flour until you have medium dough. Let rise, then make rolls. Let rise again and bake at 350 degrees 20-30 minutes.

KENTUCKY ANGEL BISCUITS

1 Pkg. Yeast
1 Tsp. Salt
½ Cup Warm Water
3 Tbsp. Sugar
5 Cups Flour
¾ Cup Shortening
1 Tsp. Baking Soda
2 Cups Buttermilk
1 Tsp. Baking Powder

Dissolve yeast in warm water. When dissolved, add flour, soda, baking powder, salt, sugar, shortening and buttermilk. Mix well and store in tight bowl in refrigerator. Pinch off what you need for a meal, let rise and bake. You don't have to let dough rise before storing in refrigerator. Bake at 450 degrees for 20 minutes. Dough stays good in refrigerator for up to a week.

REFRIGERATOR ROLLS

1 Pkg. Yeast
½ Cup Warm Water
½ Cup Butter
½ Cup Sugar
2 Tsp. Salt
1 Cup Boiling Water
1 Cup Cold Water
2 Eggs
8-9 Cups Flour

Soak yeast in ½ cup warm water. Place butter, sugar and salt in large bowl; add boiling water, when butter is melted add cold water, eggs and yeast. Stir in flour. Put into grease bowl cover and store in refrigerator. Make rolls as needed, let rise until double and bake at 425 degrees for 15 – 25 minutes.

MOMINNIE'S HOMEMADE BREAD

5 Lbs. Four
¼ Cup Sugar
2 Pkg. Yeast
4 Heaping Tbsp. Salt
6-7 Cups Water
½ Cup Shortening

Place flour in a large bowl and make hole in center. Add sugar, salt, shortening and four cups water. Mix. Dissolve yeast in one cup lukewarm water. Add to first mixture then add rest of water, enough to make dough sticky. Turn out on heavily floured board. Knead till smooth and satiny. Place in large bowl, cover and let rise until double. Punch down, let rise again till double. Make out into rolls, bread or cinnamon rolls. Let rise. Bake in well –greased pan. Makes 4-5 loaves

CINNAMON ROLLS

¼ Cup Warm Water
¼ Cup Butter Softened
¼ Cup Butter Melted
1 Cup Brown Sugar
1 Pkg. Instant Vanilla Pudding
4 Tsp. Cinnamon

1 Cup Warm Milk
¾ Cup Chopped Pecans
1 Egg Room Temperature
4 Oz. Cream Cheese Softened
1 Tbsp. Sugar
¼ Cup Butter Softened
½ Tsp. Salt
1 Cup Powdered Sugar
4 Cups Flour
½ Tsp. Vanilla
1 Pkg. Yeast
1 ½ Tsp. Milk

Combine warm water and yeast in a small bowl and set aside. Combine melted butter, pudding, warm milk, egg, 1 Tbsp. sugar, salt, flour and yeast, mix until dough is well blended. Let rise until double in size then place on a floured surface and knead lightly. Roll dough into a 17x10 inch triangle; Spread with softened butter. In a small bowl stir together brown sugar, cinnamon and pecans. Sprinkle brown sugar mixture over dough. Roll up, beginning with long side. Slice into 16 one inch slices and place in a 9x13 buttered pan. Let rise in a warm place until doubled, about 45 minutes. Preheat oven to 350 degrees and bake for 15-20 minutes. While rolls are baking stir together cream cheese, softened butter, powdered sugar, vanilla and milk. Remove rolls from oven and top with frosting.

If using a bread machine: In the pan of your bread machine, combine water, melted butter, pudding, warm milk, egg, 1 Tbsp. sugar, salt, flour, and yeast. Set machine to Dough cycle; press start. When dough cycle has finished, turn dough out a floured surface and continue as listed above.

BISCUITS

3 Cups Flour
2/3 Cup Shortening
3 Tsp. Baking Powder
1 Tsp. Salt
Milk

Mix flour and shortening with a fork until well blended. Add baking powder and salt; stir in enough milk to make a sticky dough. Dump on a floured surface and lightly knead. Pinch off or cut out and place in a greased pan or iron skillet and bake at 375 degrees 20-25 minutes or until brown.

CORNBREAD

1 Cup Cornmeal
1 ¼ Cup Flour
1 Egg
1 Cup Milk
½ Cup Shortening
¼ Cup Sugar
2 Tsp. Baking Powder

Mix all ingredients until well blended Pour into a greased cake pan or iron skillet and bake at 375 degrees until golden brown.

COWBOY BISCUITS

5 Cups Flour
½ Cup Shortening
4 Tsp. Baking Powder
2 Pkg. Yeast
1 Tsp. Salt
1 Cup Warm Water
½ Tsp. Baking Soda
2 Cups Butter Milk
½ Cup Sugar
1 Stick Melted Butter

Dissolve yeast in water. Sift together flour, baking powder, salt, baking soda and sugar. Cut in shortening. Add cup of yeast water and butter milk. Knead on well-floured board, roll out to desired thickness and cut out; Butter bottom of baking pan. Dip biscuit in butter and turn over. Arrange in pan with sides almost touching; Let rise 20 minutes. Bake in preheated oven at 450 degrees for 15 minutes. Dough will keep in ice box for 8 days. Remove as much as needed and let rise for 45-60 minutes and bake.

GARLIC CHEESE BISCUITS

1 Cup Milk
¼ Cup Shredded Cheese
1/3 Cup Mayonnaise
½ Tsp. Garlic Powder
1 Tbsp. Sugar
3 Tbsp. Melted Butter
2 Cups Flour
2 Tsp. Baking Powder

In a medium bowl, combine milk, mayonnaise, sugar and flour. Beat on high speed for almost a minute, until smooth. Using a rubber bowl scraper, streak the dough with the cheese. Batter should NOT be thin enough to pour; if necessary, add only enough additional flour so batter will drop from a spoon. Drop batter into 10 paper lined tins, or knead lightly on floured surface and cut out. Melt butter and mix in garlic, and brush tops of dough. Bake for 25-30 minutes at 375 degrees. (Biscuits triple in size when baking so fill muffin tins lightly). You may also use self-rising flour in this recipe, just don't add the baking powder if you use it.

GOOD CINNAMON ROLLS

4 ½ Cups Flour
½ Cup Water
1/3 Cup Sugar
2 Eggs
1 Tsp. Salt
3 Tbsp. Butter
2 Pkg. Yeast
1 Cup Sugar
¾ Cup Milk
1 Tbsp. Cinnamon

Combine 1 cup flour, 1/3 cup sugar, salt and dissolved yeast. Heat milk, water and ½ cup butter over low heat. Add to dry ingredients 2 minutes. Add enough flour to make dough stiff. Turn on floured board; roll out and brush with melted butter. Sprinkle with cinnamon and sugar (may add chopped nuts if desired); roll up and cut in 1 inch slices and place in pan with sides touching. Let rise until double; about 45 minutes to 1 hour. Bake at 375 degrees for 20-25 minutes or until done; drizzle with powdered sugar glaze while still warm.

GLAZE

2 Cups Powdered Sugar
1 Tbsp. Butter
½ Tsp. Vanilla
Milk

Beat powdered sugar, butter, vanilla and enough milk to make thin enough to drizzle over rolls.

JUDY'S CINNAMON ROLLS

2 Pkg. Yeast
½ Cup Warm Water
8 Cups Flour
1 Pkg. Instant Vanilla Pudding
2 Cups Warm Milk
2 Eggs
½ Cup Sugar
½ Cup Oil
2 Tsp. Salt
1 Cup Brown Sugar
2 Tsp. Cinnamon
1 Cup Raisins
1 Cup Chopped Walnuts

In a small bowl mix yeast and warm water; in a large bowl combine sugar, salt, milk, eggs, oil, pudding and flour. Mix until dough is elastic consistency and smooth. Let rise until double in size; place on a flour surface and knead lightly. Roll out into a rectangle and spread with butter; sprinkle on brown sugar, cinnamon, walnuts and raisins, roll up and slice into 1-1 ½ inch slices. Place in a 9x13 inch pan and let rise until double. Bake at 350 degrees for 20-25 minutes. Glaze while warm.

FEATHER LIGHT DOUGHNUTS

2 Pkg. Yeast
1 ½ Cups Warm Milk
1 Cup Cold Mashed Potatoes
1 ½ Cups Sugar
½ Cup Oil
2 Tsp. Salt
2 Tsp. Vanilla
½ Tsp. Baking Soda

½ Tsp. Baking Powder
2 Eggs
5 ½ - 6 Cups Flour
½ Tsp. Nutmeg
Cooking Oil for Deep Frying

In a large mixing bowl, dissolve yeast in warm milk. Add potatoes, ½ cup sugar, oil, salt, vanilla, baking soda, baking powder and eggs; mix well. Add enough to form soft dough. Place in a greased bowl, turning once to grease top. Cover and let rise in a warm place until doubled, about 1 hour. Punch dough down; roll out on a floured surface to ½ inch thickness. Cut with a 3 inch doughnut cutter. Place on greased baking sheets; cover and let rise until almost doubled, about 45 minutes. Meanwhile, combine the cinnamon and remaining sugar; set aside; Heat oil in an electric skillet or deep-fat fryer to 350 degrees, fry doughnuts until golden on both sides. Drain on paper towels; roll in cinnamon and sugar while warm or dip in your favorite powdered sugar icing.

BUNDT PAN CARAMEL ROLLS

½ Pkg. Butterscotch Pudding (not instant)
½ Stick Butter Melted
2/3 Cup Brown Sugar
¼ -1/2 Cup Pecans
1 Tsp. Cinnamon
24 Rhodes frozen rolls

In bottom of Bundt pan put budding and pecans. Drop frozen rolls on top. Mix together melted butter, brown sugar and cinnamon; pour this mixture over rolls. Cover with a towel and let stand on counter overnight. In morning, preheat oven to 350 degrees. Bake for 25-30 minutes. Invert on plate.

CINNAMON RAISIN BREAD

2 Pkg. Yeast
½ Cup Butter
½ Cup Warm Water
¾ Cup Sugar
1 ½ Cups Milk or Buttermilk
2 Tsp. Baking Powder
2 Eggs

46

2 Tsp. Salt
2 Tsp. Cinnamon
1-1 ½ Cups Raisins
5-6 Cups Flour

Dissolve yeast in warm water. Add milk, eggs, 2 ½ cups flour, butter, sugar, baking powder, salt and cinnamon. Beat until smooth. Stir in enough flour to make dough easy to handle. Knead on floured surface for 5 minutes. Divide in half. Roll out; spread with butter, sprinkle with cinnamon and sugar; sprinkle on raisins and roll up; place in greased loaf pans and let rise in warm place until double. Bake at 375 degrees for 25-30 minutes. You can glaze while still warm if desired.

MEXICAN CORN BREAD

1 Cup Cornmeal
1 Cup Cream Style Corn
¾ Cup Flour
2 Eggs
½ Tsp. Soda
1 Tsp. Salt
1/3 Cup Oil
1-3 Hot Peppers Chopped
¾ Cup Grated Cheddar Cheese

Sift together dry ingredients and blend in remaining ingredients. Heat a small amount of oil in iron skillet and add batter. Bake at 400 degrees for 25 minutes. You can bake in a regular cake pan, but crust will not be as crunchy.

BUTTERY CRESCENTS

2 Pkg. Yeast
2 Cups Warm Milk
2 Eggs Lightly Beaten
¼ Cup Butter Melted
3 Tbsp. Sugar
1 Tsp. Salt
6 ½ -7 Cups Flour
Additional Butter Melted

In a large mixing bowl, dissolve yeast in warm milk. Add eggs, butter, sugar, salt and 4 cups flour. Beat until smooth. Add enough remaining flour to form medium dough. Turn onto a floured surface; knead until smooth and elastic, about 6-8 minutes. Place in a greased bowl turning once to grease top. Cover and let rise in a warm place until doubled, about 1 hour. Punch the dough down and divide in thirds. Roll each portion into a 12 inch circle; cut each circle into 12 wedges. Roll wedges from the wide end and place with pointed end down on greased baking sheets. Cover and let rise until double, about 30 minutes. Bake at 400 degrees for 14 minutes or until golden brown. Brush with butter if desired. Makes 3 dozen

HAM & CHEDDAR ROLLS

½ Cup Milk
½ Cup Water
1 Stick Butter
1 ½ Tbsp. Yeast
1 ½ Tbs. Baking Powder
½ Cup Sugar
3 ½ Cups Flour
1 ½ Cups Wheat Flour
3 Eggs

Heat together the milk, water and butter in microwave for 5 minutes. Mix yeast, baking powder, sugar, ½ cup wheat flour, 1 ½ cups flour, then add milk mixture and eggs and beat 5 minutes then add the rest of the four and mix until dough starts to lose its tackiness. Turn out on lightly floured board and knead 3 or 4 times. Roll dough out with rolling pin to about 18x14 size. Spread very lightly with softened butter. Place thinly sliced ham over top of dough. Sprinkle generously with grated cheddar cheese (3 Cups). Place a few chopped green onions over cheese. Roll jelly roll fashion and then slice about 2 ½ inch slices. Place in greased muffin tins; let rise to double in size. Brush top of rolls with beaten egg. Bake at 350 for 10 minutes; Turn pan front to back and continue baking for 3-5 minutes or until lightly brown. Let cool before removing from pan. Makes 12 rolls

PIZZA DOUGH

1 Pkg. Yeast
1 Tsp. Salt

1 ¼ Cup Warm Water
4 Cups Flour
2 Tbsp. Oil

Mix yeast, salt and flour. Add water and oil. Knead about 5 minutes and let rise until double. Makes 2-3 Crust.

MONKEY BREAD

4 Cans Biscuits
1 ½ Sticks Butter
2/3 Cup Sugar
1 Cup Brown Sugar
1 ½ Tsp. Cinnamon
1 Tsp. Cinnamon

Cut biscuits into quarters; put cinnamon and sugar into a sack and mix well; add biscuits and shake. Then place in greased Bundt cake pan. Melt together oleo, brown sugar and cinnamon; pour this over biscuits in pan. Bake at 350 degrees for 30 minutes. You can put nuts, raisins, brown sugar and butter in the bottom of the pan and a layer of biscuits that have been shook in the cinnamon and sugar, more butter, brown sugar, nuts and raisins and second layer of biscuits.

LEMON BREAD

½ Cup Shortening
½ Tsp. Salt
1 Cup Sugar
½ Cup Milk
2 Eggs
½ Cup Chopped Nuts
1 2/3 Cups Flour
Grated Peel of One Lemon
1 Tsp. Baking Powder
3 Tbsp. Butter

Cream shortening, butter and sugar, add slightly beaten eggs and blend well; Sift flour with baking powder and salt. Alternately add the flour mixture and the milk to the shortening mixture. Stir constantly. Stir in nuts and lemon peel. Bake in greased loaf pan

at 350 degrees for 1 hour. Remove from pan immediately. Combine: ¼ cup sugar and juice of 1 lemon and brush over the top of the loaf.

HAWAIIAN NUT BREAD

2 Eggs
1 Tsp. Salt
1/3 Cup Sugar
1 Cup Nuts
1/3 Cup Oil
2 Cups Flour
3 Tsp. Baking Powder
1 Cup Crushed Pineapple

Beat eggs until light; add sugar and shortening. Fold in dry ingredients. Add nuts and pineapple (drained). Bake in loaf pans 1 hour at 350 degrees.

NOTES

_____

PIES AND COBBLERS

EASY, FLAKY PIE CRUST

4 Cups Flour
1 Tbsp. White Vinegar
1 Tbsp. Sugar
1 Egg
2 Tsp. Salt
½ Cup Water
1 ¾ Cups Shortening

Mix flour, sugar and salt. Cut in shortening. Add the vinegar, egg and water, Divide into balls, roll out on floured surface. Place in pie pans and bake or fill with filling and bake. Makes 4-5 deep dish pie crust.

GRAHAM CRACKER CRUST

3 Cups Graham Cracker Crumbs
1 Stick Butter Melted
3 Tbsp. Sugar.

Mix all ingredients and press into bottom and up sides of pie plate and fill.

OREO COOKIE CRUST

1 Pkg. Oreo Cookies
¼ Cup Butter Melted

Crush cookies (I put in the food processor) and add melted butter, mix until well blended then press into pie plates.

CUSTARD PIE

3 Eggs
2 ½ Cups Milk
½ Cup Sugar
¼ Tsp. Nutmeg
½ Tsp. Salt

Beat eggs slightly; add sugar, salt and milk. Mix well and pour into unbaked 9 inch pie crust. Place in hot 450 degree oven for 10 minutes to bake sides and bottom of crust. Decrease the heat to 325 degrees and bake 30-35 minutes or until a knife inserted in the center comes out clean. For coconut custard add 1 Cup Coconut.

KENTUCKY DERBY PIE

¼ Cup Butter Melted
1 Tsp. Vanilla
½ Cup Karo Syrup
4 Eggs
½ Cup Sugar
1 Cup Chopped Pecans
½ Cup Chocolate Chips
1 Pie Shell (9 inch)

Beat eggs; add sugar and beat until light and fluffy. Blend in syrup and butter. Stir in nuts, chocolate chips and vanilla. Pour into pie crust and bake at 450 degrees for 10 minutes then reduce heat to 350 degrees and bake an additional 30 minutes.

OWN CRUST PECAN PIE

1 Pkg. Hi-Ho Crackers (Crushed)
1 Cup Sugar
3 Egg Whites
1 Tsp. Vanilla
1 Cup Pecans

Mix cracker crumbs, ½ cup sugar and pecans. In bowl beat egg whites, remaining ½ cup sugar and vanilla. Stir all together and pour in greased pie pan. Bake at 350 degrees for 30 minutes. I double this and put in 9x13 pan and cut into bars.

COCONUT CREAM PIE

2 Cups Milk
2/3 Cup Sugar
3 Tbsp. Cornstarch
1 Tbsp. Butter
1 Tsp. Vanilla
Dash of Salt
3 Beaten Egg Yolks
1 Baked Pie Crust
1 Cup Coconut

In medium saucepan combine sugar and cornstarch; add milk gradually, stirring until smooth. Cook, stirring until thick; add small amount of hot mixture to egg yolks and blend well. Add coconut and return to mixture. Cook until thick over medium heat. Blend in vanilla, butter and salt. Pour into baked pie crust, top with meringue, sprinkle coconut on top and brown at 375 degrees for 10-15 minutes.

MERINGUE

3 Egg Whites
6 Tbsp. Sugar

Beat Egg whites while gradually adding sugar until stiff peaks form. Put on top of pie, place in oven and brown.

CHOCOLATE PIE

2 ¼ Cups Milk
3 Egg Yolks
2/3 Cup Sugar
1 Tsp. Vanilla
4 Tsp. Cornstarch
1 Tsp. Butter
¼ Tsp. Salt
½ Cup Cocoa

Mix first 5 ingredients and cocoa in a medium saucepan and cook over medium heat until thick, stirring constantly. Remove from heat and add vanilla and butter. Mix well and pour in to a cooked 9 inch pie crust. Top with meringue or cool whip.

HERSHEY BAR PIE

½ Lb. Hershey Bars
½ Cup Milk
20 Large Marshmallows
8 oz. Cool Whip
1 Tsp. Vanilla
Pinch of Salt
Baked Pie Crust (9 In.)

Mix and melt Hershey bars, milk and marshmallows over low heat; stir constantly and mix well. Cool completely and fold in cool whip, vanilla and salt. Pour into bake pie crust. Chill 2 hours and serve.

DIXIE PIE

1 ½ Cups Raisins
1 Cup Butter
1 Cup Sugar
1 Cup Brown Sugar
6 Eggs
2 Tsp. Vanilla
2-4 Tsp. Cinnamon
1 Cup Chopped Nuts
1 Cup Coconut

Crust for 2 pies; Put crust in pie plates and line with double thickness of foil. Bake at 450 degrees for 10 minutes; discard foil and cool. Put raisins in a medium saucepan, cover with water and bring to a boil then remove from heat. Cream butter and sugars; beat in eggs, vanilla and cinnamon until smooth. Drain raisins; stir raisins, coconut and nuts into creamed mixture, pour into crust and bake at 350 degrees for 30-35 minutes or until set.

PUMPKIN CREAM PIE

2 Cups Milk
1 Cup Pumpkin
2 Pkg. Instant Vanilla Pudding
2 Tsp. Pumpkin Pie Spice
1 Cup Cool Whip
1 Baked Pie Crust

In medium bowl combine all ingredients until well blended; pour into pie shell and top with cool whip. Chill and serve. This is good on graham cracker crust too.

DOUBLE LAYER PUMPKIN PIE

1st Layer:

4 oz. Cream Cheese
1 Tbsp. Milk
1 Tbsp. Sugar
1 Tub Cool Whip
1 Graham Cracker Crust

Mix cream cheese, sugar and milk until well blended and smooth; stir in cool whip and pour into crust.

2nd Layer:

1 Cup Cold Milk
1 Can Pumpkin
2 Pkg. Vanilla Pudding
2 Tsp. Pumpkin Pie Spice

Mix pudding and milk until well blended; add pumpkin and spice and stir until smooth then pour over first layer; top with cool whip, chill and serve.

COCONUT & OATMEAL PIE

3 Eggs Well Beaten
1 Tbsp. Butter
¾ Cup Coconut
1 Tsp. Vanilla
¾ Cup Quick Oats
Pinch Salt
¾ Cup Sugar
¾ Cup Karo Syrup
Unbaked Pie Crust

PREHEAT oven to 350 degrees. Mix all ingredients; pour into unbaked pie shell. Bake for 30 minutes.

PEANUT BUTTER PIE

8 oz. Cream Cheese
½ Cup Peanut Butter
½ Cup Powdered Sugar
16 oz. Cool Whip
Graham Cracker Crust
15 Mini Peanut Butter Cups

Mix the cream cheese, powdered sugar and peanut butter together until smooth. Fold in ½ the cool whip; Spoon into crust. Place remaining whipped topping over the peanut butter mixture; garnish with chopped peanut butter cups. Chill for at least 2 hours or overnight before serving. You can also use Oreo crust.

OATMEAL PIE

1/3 Cup Butter Melted
3 Eggs
2/3 Cup Sugar
1 Cup Corn Syrup
¼ Tsp. Salt
1 Cup Quick Oats
1 Unbaked Pie Crust

Beat together eggs, sugar, salt, butter and syrup. Stir in oats. Pour into the pie crust and bake in preheated 350 degree oven until set, about 45 minutes to 1 hour. Let cool before cutting.

CHOCOLATE OATMEAL PIE

¼ Cup Butter
¼ Tsp. Salt
½ Cup Sugar
1 Cup Corn Syrup
¼ Cup Cocoa
3 Eggs
1 Cup Quick Oats
1 Unbaked Pie Crust

Cream together butter and sugar; stir in cocoa and salt. Stir in syrup; add eggs one at a time, stirring after each addition until blended. Stir in oats. Pour filling into pie shell. Bake at 350 degrees about 1 hour or until knife inserted in center comes out clean.

PECAN PIE

3 Eggs
¼ Cup Butter Melted
1 Cup Corn Syrup
1 Tsp. Vanilla
½ Cup Sugar
1 Cup Pecans
1 Unbaked Pie Crust

PREHEAT oven to 350 degrees. In medium bowl beat eggs well; add syrup, sugar, butter and vanilla, mix well. Put pecans in bottom of crust and pour egg mixture over then bake for 1 hour or until knife inserted in center comes out clean.

FUDGE PECAN PIE

3 Sq. Unsweetened Chocolate
2 Cups Sugar
½ Cup Butter
¼ Tsp. Salt
4 Eggs
1 Tsp. Vanilla
1 Unbaked Pie Crust
1 Cup Pecans

Melt chocolate and butter in saucepan; beat eggs. Add sugar, salt and vanilla. Stir in pecans and melted chocolate mixture. Pour into pie crust and top with 1 cup pecan halves. Bake at 350 degrees for 35-45 minutes. DO NOT OVERBAKE.

PUMPKIN PIE

3 Eggs
½ Tsp. Salt
1 Can Pumpkin
1 Can Evaporated Milk
¾ Cup Sugar
½ Tsp. Cinnamon
½ Tsp. Allspice
1 Tsp. Ginger
1 Tsp. Pumpkin Pie Spice
1 Unbaked Pie Shell

Beat eggs, pumpkin, sugar, milk and spices; Pour into pie crust and bake at 400 degrees for 15 minutes, then reduce temperature to 350 degrees and continue baking for 45 minutes or until knife inserted halfway between center and outside edge comes out clean. Cool and serve with whipped topping.

RAISIN PIE

1 ½ Cups Raisins
1 Cup Boiling Water
¼ Cup Lemon Juice
1 Tbsp. Butter
3 Tbsp. Flour
Dash of Salt
1 Cup Sugar
1 Tsp. Cinnamon
½ Tsp. Nutmeg
½ Tsp. Allspice
2 Unbaked Pie Crust

PREHEAT oven to 425 degrees. Combine sugar, flour and salt. Slowly add boiling water stirring constantly. Cook over low heat until thick and clear. Add raisins, lemon juice and butter, mix thoroughly. Pour into pastry lined pie pan; cover with top crust and bake for 25-30 minutes.

RAISIN CREAM PIE

1 Cup Raisins
½ Cup Water
2 Eggs Separated
2 Tbsp. Flour
¾ Cup Sugar
¼ Tsp. Salt
2 Tbsp. Butter
1 Cup Milk
½ Tsp. Vanilla
1 Baked 9 inch Pie Shell

Combine raisins and water in saucepan. Cook for 5 minutes, remove from heat and let stand to cool. Beat egg yolks. Combine yolks, flour, sugar, salt, butter and milk in saucepan. Cook until thickened. Stir in raisins with liquid and vanilla. Pour filling into pastry shell. Prepare meringue, using egg whites. Spread meringue on filling; Broil until lightly browned.

LAZY DAY CHERRY COBBLER

1 Cup Flour
½ Tsp. Salt
1 Cup Sugar
½ Cup Milk
1 ½ Tsp. Baking Powder
¼ Cup Butter Melted
1 Can Cherry Pie Filling
3 Tsp. Cherry Jell-O

Mix cherry pie filling and dry Jell-O, pour into 8 or 9 inch pan. Mix flour, sugar, baking powder, salt, milk and butter until well blended. Pour over filling and bake at 375 degrees for 35-45 minutes. Double the recipe for 9x13 pan.; Can use blackberries, peaches or apples if desired.

CRUMB TOPPED APPLE PIE

5 Large Apples
½ Cup Sugar
2 Tbsp. Flour
1 Tsp. Cinnamon
2 Tbsp. Lemon Juice
1 Unbaked Pie Crust

TOPPING

½ Cup Sugar
½ Cup Flour
½ Cup Butter
½ Tsp. Cinnamon

PREHEAT oven to375 degrees. Peel and slice apples into crust; combine ½ cup sugar, 2 Tbsp. flour, and cinnamon. Pour over apples; sprinkle lemon juice on top.
Cut ½ cup sugar, flour, butter and cinnamon together for topping until well blended. Should be crumbly; Sprinkle over top of pie and bake for 45 minutes to 1 hour.

BLUEBERRY PIE

3 Cups Blueberries
Dash of Salt
3 Tbsp. Flour
2 Tbsp. Lemon Juice
¾ Cup Sugar
1 Tbsp. Butter
Easy Flaky Pie Crust

Roll out crust 1/8 inch thick and fit into an 8 inch pie pan. Sort and wash blueberries. Mix flour, sugar and salt together and sprinkle about half the mixture over the bottom of the pastry; then pour in the blueberries and sprinkle rest of sugar and flour over the top. Sprinkle lemon juice over all. Dot with butter; roll more crust for the top and lay over pies, press crusts together at rim and trim off

to ½ inch from pan. Turn under edge of crust and flute or crimp, make slits in top. Brush top of crust with melted butter or egg white and sprinkle with sugar. Bake at 350 degrees 35-45 minutes or until berries are done.

BLUEBERRY APPLE CRUNCH

1 Can Apple Pie Filling
½ Cup Butter Melted
2 Cups Blueberries
1 Cup Chopped Nuts
½ Cup Sugar
2 Tbsp. Sugar
1 White Cake Mix

PREHEAT oven to 350 degrees. Spread apple filling on bottom of 9x 13 pan. Toss together blueberries and ½ cup sugar, spoon over apple filling. Sprinkle cake mix evenly over fruit and drizzle with butter. Sprinkle with chopped nuts and remaining 2 Tbsp. sugar. Bake 50-55 minutes or until golden and bubbly.

BLACKBERRY COBBLER

2 Qts. Blackberries
1-1 ½ Cups Sugar
3 Tbsp. Flour
2 Tbsp. Lemon Juice
Easy Flaky Pie Crust

Roll out enough pie crust dough to cover the bottom and sides of a 9x13 inch pan. Combine flour, sugar; pour blackberries into crust and sprinkle flour and sugar over the top. Sprinkle with lemon juice. Roll out enough dough to cover the top; press the edges of the top and bottom crust together and crimp. Make several slashes in the top, brush with beaten egg white, sprinkle with sugar and bake at 350 degrees for 45 minutes to 1 hour.

APPLE CRISP

8 Cups Slice Apples
1 ½ Cups Flour
2 Tsp. Cinnamon

1 Tsp. Nutmeg
2 Tbsp. Flour
1 Cup Quick Oats
½ Cup Sugar
½ Tsp. Baking Soda
2/3 Cup Butter
½ Tsp. Salt
1 ½ Cups Brown Sugar
1 ½ Tsp. Cinnamon

Combine first 4 ingredients and place in 13x9 pan. Combine the remaining ingredients until well blended and sprinkle over the top of the apple mixture. Bake at 350 degrees for 30-40 minutes. May use peaches, blackberries, blueberries or cherries.

FOOLPROOF MERINGUE

3 Egg Whites
Dash of Salt
1 Cup Marshmallow Crème

Beat egg whites and salt until soft peaks form. Gradually add marshmallow crème, beating until stiff peaks form. Spread over pie fully sealing to edge of crust and bake at 350 degrees for 12-15 minutes until lightly brown.

EASY FRUIT COBBLER

1 Cup Flour
½ Cup Butter
1 Cup Sugar
1 1/3 Tbsp. Baking Powder
1 Cup Milk
28 oz. Can Fruit Un-drained
Melt butter in a 2 Quart casserole dish. Combine flour, sugar and baking powder; add milk, mixing well. Pour batter over butter in casserole dish; Spoon fruit and juice on batter. Bake at 400 degrees for 30 minutes or until golden brown.

-NOTES-

MEATS AND CASSEROLES

HASH RANCHERO

1 ½ Lbs. Ground Beef
1 ½ Tsp. Black Pepper
2/3 Cup Chopped Onion
1 Tsp. Garlic
1 Lg. Green Pepper Chopped
1 Cup Tomato Juice
3 Tsp. Chili Powder
2 Cups Cooked Rice
2 Tsp. Salt

Brown hamburger and drain; add all other ingredients and mix well. Place in a casserole dish and bake at 350 degrees for 30-40 minutes.

DEVILED STEAK STRIPS

1 ½ Lbs. Round Steak
1 ½ Cups Water
¼ Cup Flour
½ Cup Tomato Sauce
½ Cup Chopped Onion
1 Tbsp. Vinegar
1 Clove Minced Garlic
1 Tsp. Horseradish
3 Tbsp. Shortening
1 Tsp. Mustard
Salt and Pepper to Taste

Cut meat in strips, 2 or so inches long. Coat with flour; melt shortening in skillet, brown meat, onion and garlic. Add 1 Cup water, tomato sauce, vinegar, horseradish, mustard, salt and pepper. Cover and simmer 1 hour or until meat is done. Stir in remaining water and heat through. Serve over noodles or rice.

PORCUPINE MEATBALLS

1 Lb. Hamburger
½ Tsp. Pepper
¼ Cup Onion Chopped
1/3 Cup Rice
¼ Cup Celery
1 Egg
1 Tsp. Salt

½ Tsp. Garlic
½ Pkg. Saltine Crackers Crushed

Mix all ingredients and form into balls; brown in skillet and pour off grease. Add 1 pint tomato juice, ½ cup brown sugar and water to cover; cook in covered skillet or in oven for 1 hour or until done.

TATER TOT CASSEROLE

1 Lb. Hamburger
16 oz. Tater Tots
1 Can Mushroom Soup
¼ Cup Onion
4 oz. Mozzarella Cheese
Salt and Pepper to taste

Brown meat and onion; add salt and pepper. Drain meat and add soup; put in casserole dish and top with tater tots and cheese. Cover and bake at 350 degrees for 30-45 minutes. Uncover last 5 minutes.

TATER TOT TACO CASSEROLE

1 Lb. Hamburger
16 oz. Tater Tots
¼ Cup Black Olives
1 Cup Cheddar Cheese shredded
1 Pkg. Taco Seasoning
2 Tbsp. Taco Sauce
1 Cup Water
10 oz. Shredded Lettuce
1 Can Diced Tomatoes-
¼ Cup Sour Cream
1 Can Green Chiles, drained

PREHEAT oven to 350 degrees; Place tater tots in bottom of 9x 13 pan; bake for about 20 minutes or until crisp and cooked through. Cook hamburger in a large skillet until done; drain and stir in taco seasoning and water. Reduce heat to low and simmer until sauce is reduced and thick, about 10 minutes. Spoon cooked hamburger over tater tots. Pour nacho cheese dip evenly over the beef. Top with canned tomatoes, olives, ½ cup cheese and taco sauce. Bake in oven until cheese is melted and the casserole is warmed through, about 15 minutes. Remove from oven and top with remaining ½ cup of cheese. Serve atop shredded lettuce and garnish with sour cream.

TACO CASSEROLE

2 Lb. Hamburger
2 Pkg. Taco Seasoning
2 Cans Refried Beans
1 Bag Corn Chips
1 Can Enchilada Sauce
1 Can Tomato Sauce
16 oz. Shredded Cheese

PREHEAT oven to 350 degrees. Brown and drain hamburger, stir in taco seasoning. Mix half the tomato and enchilada sauce with the beans. Grease a 13x9 casserole dish and cover the bottom with corn chips. Add remaining sauces with meat; layer meat mixture, beans, cheese then more corn chips ; Bake for 30-40 minutes, sprinkle with cheese and return to oven until cheese melts.

TORTILLA CHICKEN CASSEROLE

1 Sm. Onion Chopped
2 Cups Cooked Chicken Cubed
2 Tbsp. Butter
12 Corn Tortillas, Torn
1 Can Crm. Mushroom Soup
2 Cups Shredded Cheese
1 Can Crm. Chicken Soup
1 Can Ro-Tel

PREHEAT oven to 325 degrees. In large saucepan, cook onion in melted butter until soft, not brown. Add both soups, Ro-Tel and chicken; mix well. Spray a 9x13 pan with cooking spray. Layer ingredients in the following order; tortillas, soup mix, cheese; repeat making 3 layers, ending with cheese. Bake for 40 minutes or until hot and bubbling.

SEVEN LAYER CASSEROLE

Layer in greased 9x13 pan:
2 Cups Cooked Rice
1 Tsp. Salt
1 Sliced Onion
1 Chopped Green Pepper
1 Can Corn Drained
½ Large Jar Spaghetti Sauce
2 Lb. Browned Hamburger
½ Large Jar Spaghetti Sauce

Bake covered 30 minutes at 350 degrees. You can use spaghetti or noodles instead of rice. Sprinkle top with parmesan cheese.

BISCUIT & GRAVY CASSEROLE

4-6 Cups Sausage Gravy
1 Dozen Scrambled Eggs
1 Lb. Cooked Bacon
1 Bag O'Brien Potatoes
1 Can Grand Biscuits

To make gravy, crumble and brown 1 lb. sausage in skillet; add 1 Tbsp. shortening and ¾ cup flour, or enough to make a thick paste, salt and pepper to taste, then slowly add milk stirring constantly until desired consistency is reached and gravy comes to a boil. Fry potatoes in skillet with 1-2 Tbsp. oil then place in the bottom of a 9x13 pan; top with ½ the gravy, the eggs, then bacon, more gravy. Cut biscuits in 4 pieces and place on top of the gravy with points sticking up and bake in 350 degree oven for 25 minutes or until biscuits are done.

BREAKFAST CASSEROLE

4 Cups Thawed Hash Browns
3 Tbsp. Butter
Salt and Pepper to Taste
1 Cup Shredded Cheese
¾ Lb. Cubed Ham
4-6 Eggs
1 ½ Cup Milk

Grease 9x13 pan. Spread thawed hash browns in bottom of dish. Sprinkle on salt and pepper. Put ham on top of potatoes; Dot butter on top of ham and potatoes; Sprinkle cheese on top. Beat eggs with milk and pour over top. Bake at 350 degrees for 1 hour. This can be put together the night before and put in refrigerator until morning. You can also substitute sausage for the ham.

BRUNCH CASSEROLE

12-18 Eggs
2 Cups Cheddar Cheese
1 Bag O'Brien Potatoes
1 Cup Sausage
Salt and Pepper to Taste
1 Cup Crumbled Bacon
1 Cup Diced Ham

Use any combination of meats that you prefer one, two or all three. Mix all ingredients until well blended, pour into a greased 9x13 pan and bake at 350 degrees for 45-60 minutes.

BREAKFAST PIZZA (CASSEROLE)

1 Can Crescent rolls
5 Eggs
1 Lb. Sausage
1 Cup Milk
1 Cup Hash Browns
½ Tsp. Salt
¾ Cup Cheddar Cheese
½ Tsp. Pepper
¾ Cup Mozzarella Cheese
2 Tbsp. Parmesan Cheese

Unroll rolls and flatten on sheet cake pan. Brown sausage; spread on crust. Cover with frozen hash browns. Beat eggs; add milk, salt, pepper and shredded cheeses. Pour over sausage and potatoes. Sprinkle parmesan on top. Put foil around edge for the first 15 minutes. Bake at 375 degrees for 25-30 minutes.

CROCKPOT ENCHILADA DINNER

1 Lb. Hamburger
1 Can Pinto Beans Drained
½ Cup Chopped Onion
½ Cup Sliced Black Olives
1 Can Enchilada Sauce
2 Tsp. Chili Powder
1 Can Cheese Soup
1 Tsp. Garlic Salt
1 Can Crm. Mushroom Soup
3 Large Corn Tortillas
1 Can Corn Drained
½ Cup Grated Cheese

Brown hamburger and drain; add all ingredients except tortillas and cheese. Mix well. Place one tortilla in the bottom of crock pot. Spoon one fourth of the ground beef mixture over tortilla, sprinkle with cheese. Repeat layers until all ingredients are used, ending with cheese. Cook on low for 8 hours.

PORK TENDERLOIN IN MUSHROOM SAUCE

1 ½ Lbs. Tenderloin
2 Tbsp. Shortening
1 Chicken Bouillon Cube
Salt and Pepper to Taste
1 ¾ Cups Water
½ Tsp. Oregano
½ Cup Chopped Onion
2 Tbsp. Flour
½ Cup Sliced Mushrooms
¼ Cup White Cooking Wine
4 Tbsp. Chopped Green Pepper

Cut meat into ¾ inch pieces; brown in melted shortening on both cup boiling water. Add onions, green pepper, mushrooms, bouillon, salt, pepper and oregano to browned meat. Cover and simmer 1 hour until tender. Combine flour and ¼ cup water until smooth. Stir into cooking liquid. Cook, stirring constantly until smooth and thick; add wine. Simmer 5 more minutes. Serve on rice, noodles or mashed potatoes.

PORK CHOP POTATO BAKE

6 Pork Chops
24 oz. Thawed Hash Browns
1 Can Celery Soup
1 Can Cheese Soup
½ Cup Milk
1 Can French Fried Onions
½ Cup Sour Cream
Seasoning Salt and Pepper
1 Cup Grated Cheese

Brown pork chops in lightly greased skillet. Sprinkle with seasoning salt and set aside. Combine soup, milk, sour cream, pepper and ½ tsp. seasoning salt; stir in hash browns, ½ cup grated cheese, ½ can onions. Put hash brown mixture in 9x13 pan; arrange pork chops over potatoes. Bake covered at 350 degrees for about 1 hour. Top with remaining ½ cup cheese and onions, bake uncovered about 5 minutes longer.

CASHEW CHICKEN

½ Lb. Chicken Breast per Person
Egg and Flour to roll chicken in

Remove raw chicken from bone and cut into small pieces. Flour well, roll in egg and then the flour again. Fry in hot oil. Keep warm in a covered pan in the oven.

SAUCE

Make according to number of servings, one each of the following per serving:

½ Cup Chicken Broth
1 Tsp. Sugar
1 Tbsp. Soy Sauce
2 Tsp. Cornstarch
¼ Cup Sliced celery
½ Cup Salted Cashews
½ Cup Chopped Green Onion

Heat broth; Stir in other ingredients. Reheat until thickened. Serve with chicken over steamed rice. Add soy sauce to taste.

FRIED CHICKEN

1 Cut Up Fryer
3 Cups Flour
2 or so Cups Shortening
2 Tsp. Seasoning Salt
2 Tsp. Paprika
2 Tsp. Black Pepper
1 egg
2 Cups Water

Put shortening in large skillet to melt; mix flour, salt, paprika and pepper. In another bowl combine egg and water, whisk until well blended. Dip chicken in water, then in flour; place in prepared skillet with shortening and fry slowly for 15-20 minutes, turning occasionally until done.

For chicken gravy, remove cooked chicken and part of shortening, leaving the scraps and about ½ cup shortening in the bottom of skillet. Add enough flour to make a thick paste. Add salt and pepper to taste. Add about 3 cups of milk and stir continuously until bubbling. Add more milk if necessary to desired consistency. Serve on mashed potatoes or biscuits.

MEATLOAF

3 Lbs. Hamburger
2 Pkg. Crackers Crushed
3 Eggs
1 Medium Onion Chopped
1 Green Pepper Chopped
1 Can Tomato Sauce
2 Tsp. Salt
2 Tsp. Black Pepper
4 Tbsp. BBQ Sauce
2 Tbsp. Steak Sauce

In a large bowl combine all ingredients until well mixed. Form into a loaf and place in a 9x13 pan. Top with ketchup or topping of your choice and bake at 350 degrees for 1 ½ hours or until done.

CHICKEN RICE CASSEROLE

3 Cooked Chicken Breast

2 Cups Cooked Rice
1 Pkg. California B lend Veg.
1 Can Cream Chicken Soup
1 Can Cream Celery Soup
1 Medium Onion Chopped
¼ Lb. Velveeta Cubed
1 ½ Cup Water
Salt & Pepper to Taste

Cube chicken breast and mix with all remaining ingredients. Place in a 9x13 inch pan and bake covered for 1 hour at 350 degrees. Check every 20 minutes to see if you need to add more liquid.

COWBOY CASSEROLE

2 Lbs. Hamburger
1 Can Tomatoes
1 Onion Chopped
2 Tbsp. Flour
6 Potatoes Sliced
1 Can Red Beans
1 Tsp. Garlic Powder
3Tsp. Salt
2 Tsp. Black Pepper

Brown and drain hamburger. Mix can of tomatoes and flour, set aside. Place chopped onion in the bottom of a crock pot, layer with ground beef, sliced potatoes and beans, spread tomato mixture over all. Sprinkle with seasonings, cover and cook on low for 7-9 hours.

REUBEN CASSEROLE

1 Can Sauerkraut Drained
¾ Cup Miracle Whip
1 Lb. Cooked Corned Beef
¾ Cup 1000 Island Dressing
2 Cups Swiss Cheese
4 Tbsp. Butter Melted
Shredded
1 Cup Rye Bread Crumbs

Place sauerkraut in a 2 quart glass casserole. Top with corned beef and grated Swiss cheese. Mix miracle whip and Thousand Island dressing and spread over cheese. Top with bread crumbs that have been tossed with the butter. Bake at 350 degrees for 45 minutes.

BROCCOLI CORN CASSEROLE

10 oz. Frozen Broccoli
1 Can Cream Style Corn
1 Egg
1 ½ Cups Stuffing Mix
½ Cup Melted Butter

In a large bowl, combine the broccoli, corn and egg. Put in a greased 1 quart baking dish. Sprinkle with stuffing mix and drizzle with butter. Bake uncovered at 350 degrees for 30-35 minutes or until golden brown and bubbly

TENDERLOIN

1 Whole Tenderloin
1 Onion
2 Tbsp. Oil
Seasoning Salt
1 Can Cream Mushroom Soup
1 Can Cream of Celery Soup
Salt & Pepper to Taste

Cut tenderloin in 1 ½ inch slices then sprinkle with seasoning salt and brown in oil. Place in 9x13 pan and set aside. Combine the soups, 1 ½ cans of water and salt & pepper; pour over the meat. Cover and cook at 325 degrees for 2 ½ hours.

BBQ BRISKET

1 5-6 Lb. Brisket
Salt
Garlic Powder
Pepper
1 Onion Sliced

Sprinkle brisket with seasonings; place onion slices on top and wrap tightly in foil. Bake at 325 for 4-5 hours, remove from oven and let cool. Trim off all fat and slice. Place in a 9x13 pan and cover with BBQ Sauce, cover and bake at 325 degrees for 1-1 ½ hours.

DEER SUMMER SAUSAGE

5 Lbs. Deer Burger
5 Tsp. Tender Quick Salt
4 Tsp. Peppercorns
2 ½ Tsp. Garlic Powder
3 ½ Tsp. Mustard Seed
3 Tsp. Liquid Smoke

Combine all ingredients and let set covered in the refrigerator overnight. Form into rolls, wrap in foil and bake at 200 degrees for 6-10 hours. You can add cubed cheddar cheese and chopped jalapeno peppers.

NO PEEK CHICKEN

1 Cut up Chicken
1 Can Cream Mushroom Soup
1 Can Cream Celery Soup
½ Can Milk
1 Cup Uncooked Rice
1 Pkg. Onion Soup Mix
4 Tbsp. Butter

Dot butter in bottom of 9x13 pan. Cover with rice. Mix soups and milk together and pour over rice. Place chicken on top and sprinkle with onion soup mix. Cover with 2 layers of foil and seal. Bake at 325 degrees for 2 ½ hours; DO NOT UNCOVER UNTIL YOU TAKE IT OUT OF THE OVEN!!!!

POT ROAST

4-5 Lb. Roast
3-4 Tbsp. Flour
2 Tsp. Salt
¼ Cup Oil
1 Tsp. Pepper
1 Onion Chunked
½ Tsp. Paprika
5-6 Potatoes Quartered
1 Tsp. Garlic Powder
1 Lb. Carrots Chopped

Mix flour, salt, pepper, garlic and paprika in a small bowl. Rub mixture all over roast, then sprinkle with flour, Brown in hot oil on all sides. Transfer meat to a roasting pan with some water in the bottom. Add onions, cover and bake at 350 degrees until tender. About 1 hour before roast is done add potatoes and carrots. Cook until vegetables are tender.

WEIGHT WATCHER TUNA MARINADE

1 Can Tuna Drained
½ Cup Sliced Mushrooms
¼ Cup Chopped Green Pepper
1 Sliced Tomato
¼ Cup Sliced Onion
½ Sliced Cucumber
Lettuce

MARINADE:

2 Tbsp. Vinegar
¼ Tsp. Basil
2 Tbsp. Oil
1/8 Tsp. Salt
1/16 Tsp. Dry Mustard
1/8 Tsp. Garlic Salt
1/16 Tsp. Pepper
1/8 Tsp. Onion Salt
¼ Tsp. Oregano
Dash of Cayenne Pepper

Combine marinade ingredients. Pour over tuna and green pepper in small bowl. Chill at least one hour. Spoon over other vegetables; Serves 2

CHEESY CHICKEN WITH STUFFING

4 Lb. Chicken Breast
½ Tsp. Pepper
1 Cup Bread Crumbs
2 Cans Cream Mushroom Soup
1 Cup Parmesan Cheese
1 Cup Milk
1 Tsp. Oregano
½ Tsp. Paprika
1 Tsp. Garlic Powder

1 Tsp. Salt
1 Box Stove Top Stuffing

Combine bread crumbs, ½ Cup parmesan cheese, oregano, garlic powder, salt and pepper. Roll chicken in this mixture. Place chicken in baking dish skin side down. Bake at 400 degrees for 20 minutes. Turn and continue baking for 20 minutes longer. Blend soup and milk, pour over chicken. Sprinkle with remaining parmesan cheese and paprika; bake 20 minutes more. Prepare Stove Top Stuffing as directed and serve chicken over stuffing.

BUBBLE PIZZA

2 Cans Biscuits
2 Jars Pizza Sauce
2 Lbs. Ground Beef
½ Cup Chopped Green Pepper
½ Cup Chopped Onion
Pepperoni to Taste
Mozzarella Cheese

Grease bottom of 13x9 pan. Cut biscuits in ¼; line bottom of pan with biscuits. Brown and drain ground beef; Sauté peppers and onions. Mix beef, peppers and onions with pizza sauce; stir in pepperoni and any other ingredients you like in pizza (i.e. mushrooms, olives etc.). Pour over biscuits and bake for 25-30 minutes at 350 degrees. Spread grated mozzarella cheese on top last 10 minutes or until melted.

BEEF STROGANOFF

2 Lbs. Hamburger
1 Sm. Onion Diced
4 Cups Brown Gravy
1 Can Sliced Mushrooms
1 Tsp. Garlic Powder
Salt & Pepper to Taste
1 Bag Egg Noodles
1-1 ½ Cups Sour Cream

Place hamburger and onions in large skillet; add salt, pepper and garlic powder; cook until hamburger is done; drain. In medium sauce pan make brown gravy using mix or 6 bouillon cubes in 4 cups of water, when boiling slowly whisk in 2 tablespoons of cornstarch that has been thinned with water until a thick consistency is reached. Add to hamburger and stir until well blended. Cook noodles in boiling salt water until done; then drain and stir in 2 tsp. of butter. Stir sour cream into hamburger and gravy mixture and serve over noodles.

SWISS STEAK

1-3 Lbs. Round Steak
1 Cup Flour
2   Tsp. Salt
3   1 Tsp. Pepper
1 Tsp. Garlic Powder
¼ Cup Oil
2 Cups Sliced Green Pepper
1 Cup Chopped Onion
2 Can Diced Tomatoes
1 Can Tomato Sauce

Mix flour, salt, pepper and garlic powder in a medium bowl Cut round steak into serving size pieces and dredge in flour. Heat oil in heavy skillet and cook steak until well browned or done. Place in 13x9 pan and place green pepper and onions on top. Mix diced tomatoes and sauce then pour over meat. Cover with foil and bake at 350 degrees for 1 – 1 ½ hours.

HAM AND BEANS

1 Lb. Bag of Beans
1 ½ Cups Diced Ham
4   Tbsp. Bacon Grease
5   Salt & Pepper to Taste
Water

Look beans and take out bad ones and rocks. Put in large pot; wash well and fill pot about ¾ full of water. Bring to a boil and pepper. Continue cooking until beans are done, about 2 ½ - 3 hours. Check often and keep covered with water.

SHRIMP CREOLE
4 Tbsp. Butter
1 ½ Cup Hot Water
4 Tbsp. Flour
1 ½ Tsp. Salt
1 Cup Chopped Green Onion
¼ Tsp. Cayenne Pepper
½ Cup Diced Celery
½ Tsp. Hot Pepper Sauce
½ Cup Chopped Green Pepper
½ Tsp. Thyme
2 Tbsp. Chopped Parsley
1 Bay Leaf
1 Clove Garlic Crushed
Bring to a full boil and add shrimp. Stir and bring to a second full boil. Cook until shrimp are done (shrimp should be pink). Remove from heat and serve over cooked rice.

1 Tsp. Sugar
8 oz. Tomato Sauce
2 Lbs. Raw Shrimp
1 Can Diced Tomatoes
Cooked Rice

Melt butter in large skillet. Make a roué by stirring in flour slow and cooking over low heat until golden brown. Add onion, celery, green pepper, parsley and garlic. Cook stirring constantly 5 minutes. Stir in remaining ingredients except the shrimp and rice. Cover and simmer for 30 minutes, stirring occasionally.

NOTES

SALADS

APPLE SALAD

3-4 Apples Chopped
1 ½ Cups Mini Marshmallows
1 ½ Cups Raisins
1 Cup Crushed Pineapple
1 Cup Miracle Whip
2 Tbsp. Sugar
1 Cup Chopped Nuts

Wash and chop unpeeled apples; add raisins, nuts, pineapple, and marshmallows; mix in miracle whip and sugar. Stir until well blended, store in refrigerator.

APPLE SNICKER SALAD

4 Apples
Grapes (optional)
4 oz. Sour Cream
Mini Marshmallows (optional)
6 oz. Cool Whip
3 Snicker Bars Chopped

Cut apples into bite size pieces, leaving skin on the apple. Chop Snickers into small chunks. In a medium size bowl, mix sour cream and cool whip together. Add apples, Snickers and grapes or marshmallows; stir until well blended; cover and store in refrigerator.

BROCCOLI-CAULIFLOWER SALAD

1 Head Cauliflower Chopped
1 ½ Cup Shredded Cheese
1 Head Broccoli Chopped
½ Red Onion Chopped
1 Can Sliced Black Olives
1 Green Pepper Chopped
Bacon Bits

Mix cauliflower, broccoli, onions, olives, cheese, peppers and bacon bits. Set aside while making dressing.

DRESSING

1 Cup Miracle Whip

2 Tbsp. Vinegar
½ Cup Sugar

Mix all ingredients until well blended then pour over salad.

6 CUP SALAD

1 Cup Coconut
1 Cup Mini Marshmallows
1 Cup Pineapple Drained
1 Cup Pecans
1 Cup Mandarin Oranges
1 Cup Cool Whip

Drain oranges and pineapple. Mix together, coconut, pineapple, mandarin oranges, marshmallows, and pecans. Fold in cool whip. Refrigerate until chilled

FRUIT SALAD

1 Can Sliced Peaches
1 Can Pineapple Chunks
1 Can Pears
1 Can Mandarin Oranges
1 Can Fruit Cocktail
1 Can Tropical Fruit
2 Apples Chopped
3 Bananas Sliced
1 Box French Vanilla Pudding
1 Jar Maraschino Cherries

Drain all fruit and mix with apples and bananas; stir in dry vanilla pudding and maraschino cherries until well blended. You can add coconut and/or nuts if desired.

ORANGE SALAD

1 Pkg. Orange Jell-O
1 Instant Vanilla Pudding
1 ¼ Cups Hot Water
1 Sm. Can Crushed Pineapple
1 Sm. Carton Cool Whip

Mix Jell-O, pudding mix and hot water; stir well and let set up. Add pineapple and oranges. Fold in cool whip and chill.

BROCCOLI SALAD

1 Head Broccoli
1 Head Cauliflower
1 Lb. Fried Bacon Crumbled
¼ Cup Sugar
8 oz. Shredded Cheese
¼ Tsp. Salt
½ Cup Chopped Red Onion
½ Cup Sunflower Seeds
2 Cups Miracle Whip
2 Tbsp. Vinegar

Combine 2 Cups Miracle Whip, sugar, salt and vinegar n a large bowl: Clean, rinse and cut broccoli and cauliflower to desired size. Stir into miracle whip mixture. Add cheese and onion to mixture and stir. Chill in refrigerator; just before serving top with fried bacon crumbs and sunflower seeds.

SPAGHETTI SALAD

1 Lb. Spaghetti
1 Yellow Bell Pepper Diced
1 Bottle Italian Dressing
1 Red Bell Pepper Diced
1 Pkg. Dry Italian Seasoning
Summer Sausage Diced
1 Medium Cucumber Diced
1 Purple Onion Diced
1 Pint Cherry Tomatoes
Sliced Mushrooms (optional)

Cook spaghetti according to package, rinse in cold water, set aside. In a large bowl, add noodles, dressing, dry dressing, veggies and meat, mix well. Chill until ready to serve. You can use salami or pepperoni instead of summer sausage.

CHERRY FLUFF SALAD

1 Can Cherry Pie Filling

1 Can Eagle Brand Milk
1 Can Crushed Pineapple
2 Cups Mini Marshmallows
1 Tub Cool Whip

Drain pineapple. In a large bowl combine cherry pie filling, pineapple, marshmallows, milk and nuts; stir until well blended, fold in cool whip.

GREEN JELL-O SALAD

2 ½ Cups Crushed Pineapple
6 oz. Cream Cheese
1 Pkg. Lime Jell-O
2 Cups Cool Whip
1 Cup Diced Celery
1 Cup Chopped Pecans

Do not drain pineapple. Heat pineapple to boiling, add Jell-O and stir to dissolve. Chill until partially set. Soften cream cheese and add to gelatin mixture and blend. Fold in cool whip, celery and nuts. Chill until firm.

PINEAPPLE-LIME SALAD

1 Can Crushed Pineapple
1 Sm. Tub Cool Whip
1 Large Pkg. Lime Jell-O
½ Cup Chopped Nuts
1 Sm. Carton Cottage Cheese
½ Cup Marshmallows

Mix pineapple (with juice) and Jell-O together in pan and bring to a boil. Cool. Fold in cottage cheese, cool whip, nuts and marshmallows. Chill until set.

PEA SALAD

3 Cans Peas Drained
1 Lb. Diced Cheese (Colby)
1 Onion Diced
4 Boiled Eggs
4 Dill Pickles Chopped
1 Cup Miracle Whip
Salt and Pepper to Taste

1 Tbsp. Sugar
3 Slices Crumbled Bacon
1 Tsp. Mustard

Fry bacon and crumble. Drain peas and put in medium bowl; add remainder of ingredients and stir until well blended. Cover and put in refrigerator to chill. Sprinkle with bacon just before serving.

ELEGANT SALAD

1 Head Lettuce Shredded
4 Cups Miracle Whip
1 Diced Onion
1 Cup Sour Cream
3-4 Stalks Diced Celery
4 Tbsp. Sugar
1 Green Pepper Chopped
6 oz. Shredded Cheese
1 Sm. Bag Frozen Peas
6 Slices Fried Bacon Crumbled

In 13x9 dish put lettuce in the bottom, layer of onions (can use green onions), layer of celery, layer of green pepper, and layer of frozen peas. (I put a layer of broccoli & cauliflower also). Mix Miracle Whip, sour cream and sugar then spread over top of the salad, sealing to edges. Sprinkle cheese on top, then crumbled bacon. Chill until ready to serve.

PRETZEL BASE SALAD

2 Cups Crushed Pretzels
½ Cup Powdered Sugar
¾ Cup Melted Butter
2 Cups Mini Marshmallows
3 Tbsp. Sugar
2 Pkg. Strawberry Jell-O
1 Tub Cool Whip
2 ½ Cups Boiling Water
8 oz. Cream Cheese
10 oz. Pkg. Strawberries

First Layer:

Mix pretzels with margarine and sugar. Place in a 9x13 pan and bake at 325 degrees for 15 minutes. Cool completely.

Second Layer:

Mix cool whip with cream cheese and powdered sugar, then fold in marshmallows. Spread this over the pretzel layer.

Third Layer:

Dissolve strawberry Jell-O in boiling water, when partially set add strawberries and pour over second layer. Put in refrigerator until set. Cover top with cool whip and sprinkle with pretzel crumbs or nuts.

ORANGE TAPIOCA SALAD

2 Boxes Tapioca Pudding
1 Cup Mini Marshmallows
1 Pkg. Orange Jell-O
1 Sm. Tub Cool Whip
3 Cups Hot Water
1 Can Mandarin Oranges

Cook tapioca pudding, Jell-O and water together until thick. When cool, add drained oranges, marshmallows and cool whip. Allow to chill before serving. Can use strawberry Jell-O and strawberries instead of oranges.

WATERGATE SALAD

1 Can Crushed Pineapple
1 Lrg. Tub Cool Whip
1 Instant Pistachio Pudding
2 ½ Cups Mini Marshmallows
½ Cup Pecans
½ Cup Coconut
1 Jar Maraschino Cherries Drained

Mix pineapple with juice, pudding, coconut, pecans, cherries and marshmallows. Fold in cool whip and let chill thoroughly.

VIOLETS IN THE SNOW

2 Cups Boiling Water
1 Can Blueberry Pie Filling
1 Pkg. Black Cherry Jell-O
1 Tub Cool Whip
16 oz. Fat Free Sour Cream

Mix together boiling water and Jell-O, stir until Jell-O is dissolved. Add sour cream and pie filling, stir together well. Chill until set and serve with cool whip on top.

CRANBERRY SALAD

1 Qt. Cranberries Ground
1 Box Cherry Jell-O
1 Orange Ground
2 Cups Sugar
3 Apples Ground
1 Cup Chopped Nuts

Dissolve Jell-O in ¼ water and ¼ cup orange juice that you have brought to a boil, add rest of ingredients and let set overnight.

LAYERED CHRISTMAS SALAD

1 Pkg. Lime Jell-O
1 Pkg. Strawberry Jell-O
1 Can Cranberry Sauce
8 oz. Cream Cheese

Dissolve lime Jell-O as directed on box an pour into 8x8 glass pan. Set in refrigerator until firm. After the Jell-O is firm, spread cranberry sauce on top. Next, spread softened cream cheese on top of the cranberry sauce. Chill until this is firm. Next, prepare the strawberry Jell-O as directed on box, pour this over the other 3 layers and chill until firm. This can easily be doubled and put in 13x9 pan.

SEA BREEZE SALAD

3 Pkg. Orange Jell-O
1 Can Lemon Pie Filling
2 Cups Boiling Water
1 Sm. Tub Cool Whip
2 Cups Pineapple Juice
1 Cup Pineapple Tidbits

Drain pineapple, reserve juice and add enough water to make 2 cups. Mix Jell-O, water and pineapple juice/water mixture. Chill, then add pie filling, and whip with mixer until frothy. Add cool whip and pineapple. Pour into a 9x13 pan, chill until set.

BLUEBERRY CREAM CHEESE SALAD

2 Sm. Boxes Raspberry Jell-O
1 Env. Unflavored Gelatin
8 oz. Cream Cheese
½ Cup Pecans
1 Cup Half & Half
1 Tsp. Vanilla
½ Cup Sugar
1 Can Blueberries

Prepare 1 box raspberry Jell-O as for mold. Pour into 9x9 pan; let set until firm. Mix cream, sugar and vanilla together, heat until warm, remove from heat and add soft cream cheese and beat until mixed well. Cool. Mix unflavored gelatin with ¼ cup water; add to cream cheese mixture and add pecans. Pour on top of set Jell-O; let set until firm. Prepare raspberry Jell-O with one cup boiling water; let cool a little and add blueberries with their juice. Pour on top of set cream cheese mixture and chill until set.

TUNA SALAD

2 Cans Tuna Drained
3 Hard Boiled Eggs Chopped
3-4 Dill Pickles Chopped
½ Onion Chopped
½ Cup Chopped Celery
½ Cup or so Miracle Whip

Salt & Pepper to Taste

In medium bowl combine all ingredients except miracle whip. Add miracle whip a little at a time until desired consistency is reached.

CHICKEN SALAD

2 Cup Cubed Chicken
¼ - ½ Cup Diced onion
¼ Cup Diced Celery
2/3 Cup Miracle Whip
2-3 Diced Dill Pickles

Take left over fried chicken off the bone and cube or chop; place in a medium bowl and add remainder of ingredients and stir well. You can use sweet relish instead of pickles.

STEVEN'S CHICKEN SALAD

2 Cans Chicken Drained
1 Can Pineapple Tidbits
½ Cup Slivered Almonds
½ Cup Miracle Whip

Drain chicken and pineapple; chop pineapple into small pieces. Mix all ingredients until well blended. Serve with crackers or on croissants. You can substitute any fruit you like for the pineapple, i.e. apples, grapes etc.

NOTES

SOUPS AND CHILI

BROCCOLI CHEESE SOUP

2 Tbsp. Butter Melted
1 Onion Chopped
½ Cup Butter Melted
½ Cup Flour
4 Cups Half & Half
4 Cups Chicken Stock
1 Lb. Fresh Broccoli
2 Cups Carrots Julienned
½ Tsp. Nutmeg
16 oz. Grated Sharp Cheddar
Salt & Pepper to Taste

Sauté onion in butter. Set aside. Cook melted butter and four using a whisk over medium heat for 3-5 minutes, stirring constantly and add the half and half. Add the chicken stock. Simmer for 20 minutes. Add the broccoli, carrots and onions. Cook over low heat 20-25 minutes. Add salt and pepper. Add cheese and stir in nutmeg.

POTATO SOUP

 5 Potatoes Cubed
1 Cup Celery Chopped
1 Cup Onion Chopped
1 Tbsp. Butter
1 Cup Milk
Salt & Pepper to Taste

Peel and cube potatoes and put in a saucepan along with the onions and celery. Add water to cover. Bring to a boil, lower the heat and simmer for 20-25 minutes or until potatoes are tender. Add milk and butter and reheat to boiling. Add salt and pepper.

TACO SOUP

1 Lb. Hamburger
1 Pkg. Taco Seasoning
1 Onion Chopped
1 Pkg. Ranch Dressing Mix
3 Cans Mexican Chili Beans
1 ½ Cups Water
1 Can Corn Drained

Tortilla Chips
1 Can Diced Tomatoes
Shredded Cheese
1 Can Chopped Green Chilies
Sour Cream
1 Can Tomato Sauce

Brown beef and onions in a large kettle over medium heat until meat is browned and onions are tender. Stir mixture until meat crumbles; drain. Stir in beans, corn, tomato sauce, diced tomatoes, chilies, taco seasoning, ranch dressing mix and water; bring to a boil. Reduce heat and simmer uncovered 20-25 minutes; stirring occasionally. Spoon soup into bowls; Top with shredded cheese, sour cream and crumbled tortilla chips.

CREAM OF CELERY SOUP

2 Cups Sliced Celery
¼ Cup Flour
1 Onion Diced
1 ½ Cups Chicken Broth
½ Tsp. Salt
4 ½ Cups Milk
¼ Cup Butter
1 ¼ Tsp. Salt

Cut leaves and stems of celery. Put celery and onion in a 3 quart saucepan, add water and salt, cover and simmer until tender about 10 minutes. Melt butter in another saucepan, blend in flour, add milk and cook with constant stirring until sauce boils and thickens. Now stir in the 1 ¼ Tsp. salt and the cooked vegetables with their liquid. Reheat to boiling and serve.

CHICKEN AND WILD RICE SOUP

1 Cup Wild Rice
2 Tbsp. Butter
5 ½ Cups Chicken Broth
1 ½ Cups Cooked Chicken
1 ½ Cups Sliced Mushrooms
½ Cup Onion Chopped
½ Cup Chopped Parsley
Salt and Pepper to Taste

Run cold water over rice in a strainer for 1 minute. In a large sauce pan, mix rice, butter, broth, salt and pepper. Bring to a boil; reduce heat, cover and simmer for 45 minutes. Add mushrooms, onions, chicken and parsley. Continue to boil for another 5 minutes, remove from heat and serve.

OLIVE GARDEN SOUP

1 Lb. Hamburger
1 Can Ranch Style Beans
1 Med. Onion
3 Cans Minestrone Soup
1 Can Ro-tel
1 Can Water

Brown meat and drain fat. In slow cooker put browned meat and all other ingredients. Stir well. Cook on low all day; Excellent with cornbread.

BAKED POTATO SOUP

2/3 Cup Butter
12 Strips Bacon Crumbled
2/3 Cup Flour
1 ¼ Cup Cheddar Cheese
7 Cups Milk
1 Cup Sour Cream
4 Baked Potatoes Cubed
1 Tsp. Salt
4 Green Onions Sliced
1 Tsp. Pepper

In a large pot, melt butter, stir in flour, heat and stir until smooth. Gradually add milk, stirring constantly until thickened. Add Potatoes and onions. Bring to a boil, stirring constantly. Reduce heat and simmer for 10 minutes. Add bacon, cheese, sour cream, salt and pepper and stir until cheese is melted. Serve immediately.

CHILI

3 Lbs. Hamburger
3 Cans Chili Hot Beans
2 Cans Diced Tomatoes

1 Large Onion Chopped
1 Can Tomato Juice
2 Pkg. Williams Chili Seasoning
Salt & Pepper to Taste
Cayenne Pepper (optional)

In a large pot crumble hamburger, add onion and cook until hamburger is done. Drain. Add tomatoes, beans, and chili seasoning. Pour in tomato juice a little at a time until desired thickness is reached. Add salt and pepper, cover and simmer for about 45 minutes to 1 hour. Taste and adjust salt, pepper and chili seasoning if necessary. The longer the chili simmers the better it will taste.

CLAM CHOWDER

4 Potatoes Cubed
2 Onions Chopped
½ Cup Butter
¾ Cup Flour
8 Cups Milk
4 Cans Chopped Clams
3 Tsp. Salt
1 Tsp. Sage
1 Tsp. Thyme
1 Tsp. Pepper
Place potatoes in a saucepan and cover with water; bring to a boil. Cover and cook until tender, 12-15 minutes. Meanwhile, in a soup pot, sauté onions in butter until tender. Add flour; mix until smooth. Stir in milk. Cook over medium heat, stirring constantly, until thickened and bubbly. Drain potatoes; add to kettle. Add clams and remaining ingredients; heat thoroughly.

WHITE CHILI

2 ½ Cups Water
1 Tsp. Lemon Pepper
1 Tbsp. Cumin Divided
4 Chicken Breast (skinless)
4 Cloves Minced Garlic
1 Tbsp. Olive Oil
1 Cup Chopped Onion
2 Cans White Corn

8 oz. Chilies Un-drained
1 ½ Tbsp. Lime Juice
2 Cans Great Northern Beans

In stockpot put water, lemon pepper, 1 tsp. cumin and chicken breast. Bring to a boil and simmer for 30 minutes or until chicken is done. Remove chicken and cut into 1 inch chunks and return to pot. In skillet combine garlic, onion and oil, sauté for 1 minute then add to chicken. Add drained corn, chilies, lime juice and bring to a boil then add beans. If chili is too thick add chicken broth to get desired consistency. Serve over crushed tortilla chips and sprinkle with grated Monterey Jack cheese.

STEVEN'S CHILI

2 Lbs. Hamburger
1 Large Onion Diced
3 Cans Pinto Beans Drained
3 Cans Chili Beans
2 Cans Diced Tomatoes
1 Can Tomato Paste
1 Bottle Chili Sauce
Salt & Pepper to Taste
2 Pkg. Chili Seasoning
1 Chopped Green Pepper

Cook hamburger and onion in a large skillet until hamburger is done; drain well and put in crock pot. Add beans, tomatoes, tomato paste, chili sauce, salt, pepper, seasoning and green pepper. If chili is too thick add water or tomato juice to desired consistency. Taste and adjust chili seasoning as desired.

BEEF STEW

2 Lbs. Stew Meat
2 Tbsp. Oil
2 Cups Water
1 Tsp. Garlic Powder
1 Bay Leaf
1 Onion Diced
2 Tsp. Salt
1 Tsp. Pepper

4 Carrots Sliced
3 Stalks Celery Chopped
4 Potatoes Cubed
2 Tbsp. Cornstarch
1 Tbsp. Worcestershire Sauce

Brown meat in hot oil; add water, Worcestershire sauce, garlic, bay leaf, onion, salt, and pepper. Cover and simmer for 1 ½ hours. Remove bay leaf, add carrots, celery and potatoes. Cover and cook 30-40 minutes longer. To thicken gravy, remove 2 cups hot liquid. Using a separate bowl, combine ¼ cup water and cornstarch until smooth. Mix with a little hot liquid and return mixture to pot. Stir and cook until bubbly.

VEGETABLE BEEF SOUP

8-10 Cups Beef Broth
1-2 Lbs. Stew Meat or Roast
1 Can Diced Tomatoes
1 Can Corn Drained
1 Can Tomato Sauce
1 Can Green Beans Drained
1 ½ Cups Diced Carrots
3-4 Potatoes Diced
1 Cup Celery Chopped
½ Head Cabbage Chopped
2 Tsp. Salt
1 Tsp. Pepper
1 Onion Chopped

In a large pot boil stew meat until tender, (may use leftover roast or chuck roast that you have cubed in 1 inch pieces). Add enough water to meat to make 8-10 cups of broth. Add all other ingredients and bring to a boil then reduce heat to medium, cover and simmer for 30-45 minutes. You may use any vegetables you like.

CHICKEN NOODLE SOUP

1 Whole Chicken
2 ½ Quarts Water
1 Cup Diced Carrots
1 Cup Diced Celery
1 Tbsp. Salt

4 Chicken Bouillon Cubes
¼ Cup Chopped Onion
Salt & Pepper to Taste
1 Pkg. Fine Noodles

Place chicken in a large pot and cover with water. Add salt and pepper. Boil until chicken is done, remove from the broth and let cool, then debone. Add chicken meat back to broth; add celery, carrots, onions and bouillon cubes. Bring to a boil and add noodles, turn on low and simmer 20-25 minutes. Taste and adjust salt and pepper as needed.

TURKEY VEGETABLE SOUP

6 Cups Turkey Broth
3 Potatoes Chopped
2 Carrots Chopped
2 Stalks Celery Chopped
2 Onions Chopped
2 Cans Cream Style Corn
2 Cans Lima Beans
2 Cups Cooked Turkey
1 Tsp. Chili Powder
Salt & Pepper to Taste

In a large soup pot combine broth, potatoes, carrots, celery and onions; bring to a boil. Reduce heat; cover and simmer for 30 minutes or until the vegetables are tender. Add remaining ingredients. Cover and simmer for 10 minutes or until heated through.

BEAN SOUP

1 Lb. White Beans
2 Taters Cubes
1 Slice Country Ham Cubed
Dash Red Pepper
1 Small Onion Chopped
2 Carrots Grated
Salt and Pepper to Taste

Wash beans, cover with water, add ham, salt and pepper; bring to a boil then reduce heat to low and continue to cook for 2 hours or until beans are soft. Partially mash a few beans; add vegetables and red pepper; cook another 30 minutes. If soup is too thick add more water. Serve with cornbread or corn cakes.

FRENCH ONION SOUP

6 Cups Thin Sliced Onions
1 Tbsp. Sugar
½ Tsp. Pepper
1/3 Cup Oil
6 Cups Beef Broth
8 Slices French Bread
½ Cup Shredded Cheese

In a Dutch oven, cook the onions, sugar and pepper in oil over medium-low heat for 20 minutes or until onions are caramelized, stirring frequently. Add the broth; bring to a boil. Reduce heat; cover and simmer for 30 minutes. Ladle soup in to ovenproof bowls. Top each with a slice of French bread; sprinkle with cheese. Broil 4-6 inches from heat until cheese is melted and bubbly. Serve immediately.

CHICKEN GUMBO

1 Chicken Cut Up
2 Quarts Water
¾ Cup Flour
½ Cup Oil
½ Cup Green Onions Sliced
½ Cup Chopped Green Pepper
½ Cup Chopped Red Pepper
½ Cup Chopped Celery
2 Cloves Garlic Minced
½ Lb. Smoked Sausage Diced
½ Lb. Ham Diced
½ Lb. Shrimp Peel & Devein
1 Cup Chopped Okra
1 Can Kidney Beans Drained
1½ Tsp. Salt
1 Tsp. Pepper
1 Tsp. Hot Sauce
6 Cups Cooked Rice (optional)

Place the chicken and water in a Dutch oven and bring to a boil. Reduce heat; cover and simmer 45-60 minutes or until chicken is tender, skimming the surface as foam rises. Remove chicken and set aside until cool enough to handle. Remove and discard skin and bones. Cut chicken into bite-size pieces. Strain the broth through a colander; skim the fat. Reserve 6 cups of broth. In the Dutch oven combine the flour and oil until smooth; cook and stir over medium heat for 2-3 minutes or until brown. Stir in the onions, peppers, celery and garlic; cook for 5 minutes or until vegetables are tender. Stir in the sausage, ham and reserved broth and chicken. Bring to a boil. Reduce heat; cover and simmer for 45 minutes. Add the shrimp, okra, beans, salt, pepper and hot sauce; cover and simmer for 10-15 minutes longer or until shrimp is cooked; Spoon 1 cup gumbo into bowl and top with ½ cup rice if desired.

CORN CHOWDER

1 Onion Chopped
½ Cup Butter
2 ½ Cups Water
2 Cans Cream Style Corn
4 Medium Potatoes Cubed
2 Cups Milk
1 ½ Tsp. Salt
1 Tsp. Pepper

In a large pot, sauté onion in butter until tender; add the water, corn and potatoes; bring to a boil. Reduce heat; cover and simmer for 16-20 minutes or until potatoes are tender. Reduce heat to low. Stir in the milk, salt and pepper. Cook for 5-10 minutes or until heated through, stirring occasionally.

SMOKEY CORN CHOWDER

½ Cup Chopped Onion
4 Cups Milk
4 Tbsp. Butter
12 oz. Smoked Sausage Sliced
¼ Cup Flour
1 16 oz. Can Corn Drained
1 Tsp. Salt
1 8oz. Can Lima Beans Drained
1 Tsp. Pepper

In saucepan, cook onion in butter until tender. Blend in flour, salt and pepper. Add milk all at once. Cook, stirring until thick and bubbly. Stir in sausage links, corn and beans. Simmer 15 minutes.

OYSTER SOUP

1 Can Oysters
2 Tbsp. Butter
1 Quart Milk
Salt & Pepper to Taste

Drain oysters and reserve the juice. Put reserved oyster juice, milk, butter, salt and pepper in pan over heat. When milk is hot, add oysters. Cook until oysters come to the top.

HAMBURGER VEGETABLE SOUP

1 Lb. Lean Hamburger
1 Tsp. Kitchen Bouquet
1 Cup Sliced Carrots
1 Tsp. Pepper
1 Cup Diced Celery
1 Bay Leaf (remove)
1 Cup Cubed Potatoes
¼ Tsp. Basil
2 Medium Diced Onions
3 Cups Water
1 28oz Can Tomatoes
2 Tsp. Salt

Brown hamburger and drain; add remaining ingredients. Heat to boiling and reduce heat. Cover and simmer just until vegetables are tender, about 20-25 minutes; May add 2 Tsp. of chili powder for a south of the border flavor.

NOTES

VEGGIES

SESAME ASPARAGUS

1 Lb. Fresh Asparagus
1 Clove Garlic Minced
2 Tbsp. Butter
½ Cup Chicken Broth
1 Tbsp. Sesame Seeds

In a skillet, sauté the asparagus and garlic in butter for 2 minutes; Stir in broth; bring to a boil. Reduce heat; cover and simmer for 5-6 minutes or until asparagus is crisp-tender. Remove to a serving dish and sprinkle with sesame seeds. Serve immediately. You may serve alone or with Hollandaise Sauce.

HOLLANDAISE SAUCE

½ Cup Butter
3 Large Egg Yolks
1 Tbsp. Lemon Juice
1/8 Tsp. Salt
Dash Cayenne Pepper
2 Tbsp. Hot Water

Heat butter in heavy saucepan until hot and foamy, but not browned; in a small bowl, whisk or beat egg yolks with lemon juice, salt, and cayenne pepper. Gradually beat in butter, then water. Return mixture to saucepan and beat over VERY low heat until mixture is slightly thickened. Serve immediately or let stand over warm water for up to 30 minutes. This makes about 2/3 cup of hollandaise sauce. If cooked at too high a temperature the eggs will scramble.

CRUNCHY ASPARAGUS MEDLEY

1 ½ Lbs. Fresh Asparagus
1 Cup Thin Sliced Celery
2 Cans Water Chestnuts
¼ Cup Slivered Almonds
2 Tbsp. Soy Sauce
2 Tbsp. Butter

Cut asparagus in 2 inch pieces. In a large saucepan, cook the asparagus and celery in a ½

inch of water for 3-5 minutes or until crisp-tender; drain. Stir in water chestnuts, almonds, say sauce and butter; heat through; May serve alone or with hollandaise sauce.

FRIED CABBAGE

1/4 Cup Bacon Grease
1 Tsp. Sugar
½ Tsp. Salt
¼ Tsp. Red Pepper Flakes
¼ Tsp. Pepper
6 Cups Chopped Cabbage
½ Cup Water

In a large skillet, melt bacon grease over medium heat. Stir in the sugar, salt, pepper and pepper flakes. Add the cabbage and water. Cook for 10-12 minutes or until cabbage is tender, stirring occasionally.

RUBY RED CABBAGE

1 Cup Dried Cranberries
1 Lg. Head Red Cabbage Sliced
¼ Red Wine Vinegar
¼ Cup Apple Juice
¼ Cup Plum Jelly
2 Tbsp. Brown Sugar
½ Tsp. Salt
½ Tsp. Pepper

In a Dutch oven or large saucepan, cook cranberries in butter until softened, about 3 minutes. Add the remaining ingredients, cover and cook over medium heat until cabbage is wilted, about 5-7 minutes. Transfer to a greased 2 quart baking dish. Cover and bake for 1 hour or until tender.

HAM & CABBAGE

2 Cups Diced Ham
1 Lg. Head Cabbage Chopped
¼ Cup Bacon Grease
1 Cup Water
1 ½ Tsp. Salt

1 Tsp. Pepper

In a large pot, melt bacon grease; add water, ham, cabbage, salt and pepper. Bring to a boil and reduce heat to medium-low. Continue to cook for 20-25 minutes until cabbage is tender. This is really good served with corn bread.

CORNED BEEF & CABBAGE

3-4 Lb. Corned Beef Brisket
8 Potatoes Peeled
With Spice Packet
1 Bay Leaf (Remove)
1 Head Cabbage Cut in Wedges
1 Tsp. Garlic Powder
2 Tsp. Salt
1 Tsp. Pepper

Place corned beef in a large pot or Dutch oven and cover with water. Add the spice packet that came with the corned beef, bay leaf, garlic, salt and pepper. Cover and bring to a boil, then reduce to a simmer. Cook approximately 50 minutes per pound or until tender. Remove from pot, remove the bay leaf, reserve the juice, and let cool. Slice meat across the grain. Place a layer of corned beef, layer of cabbage and layer of potatoes. Continue to layer ending with meat on top. Pour reserved juice over all, adding water if necessary to cover; bring to a boil, reduce heat and cook until potatoes are done.

OLD SETTLERS BAKED BEANS

1 Lb. Hamburger
½ Lb. Bacon Diced
1 Cup Onion Diced
½ Cup Ketchup
1 Tsp. Salt
1 Cup Brown Sugar
1 Can Pork & Beans
1 Can Kidney Beans Drained
1 Can Lima Beans Drained

Combine hamburger, bacon and onion, cook until hamburger is done. Drain well. Add catsup, salt,

brown sugar, pork & beans, lima beans, and kidney beans, mix well. Place in casserole dish and bake for 40-50 minutes at 350 degrees.

GREEN BEANS

1 Quart Green Beans
1 Sm. Onion Chopped
3 Tbsp. Bacon Grease
Salt & Pepper to Taste

Combine the ingredients in a saucepan. Bring to a boil; reduce heat and simmer for about 1 hour. You can use bacon instead of bacon grease; chop 3 pieces of bacon and fry then add to the beans.

GREEN BEAN CASSEROLE

2 Cans Green Beans
1 Tsp. Pepper
¾ Cup Milk
1 Can French Fried Onions
1 Can Cream of Mushroom Soup

Drain beans; combine beans, milk, soup, pepper and ½ can of the onions. Pour into 1 ½ quart casserole: Bake, uncovered, at 350 degrees for 30 minutes. Top with remaining onions and bake 5 minutes longer

BAKED BEANS

4 Cans Pork & Beans
1 Onion Chopped
¼ Cup BBQ Sauce
4 Tbsp. Molasses
¾ Cup Brown Sugar
½ Cup Chopped Green Pepper
2 Tbsp. Mustard

Drain pork and beans; stir in remainder of ingredients and put in a casserole dish and bake at 350 degrees for 1 hour.

GREEN BEAN & SWEET ONION GRATIN

16 oz. Frozen Green Beans

1 Lb. Vidalia Onions Sliced
¼ Cup Butter
¼ Cup Flour
½ Tsp. Salt
¼ Tsp. Pepper
Dash Nutmeg
1 Cup Chicken Broth
1 Cup Half & Half or Milk
1 ½ Cups Bread Crumbs
6 Tbsp. Parmesan Cheese
2 Tbsp. Oil

PREHEAT oven to 325 degrees. Cook frozen green beans according to package directions. Meanwhile slice onions thin and place in medium saucepan and boil in a small amount of water for 4-5 minutes or until tender. Drain in a colander and set aside. For sauce, in the same saucepan, melt butter. Stir in flour, salt, pepper and nutmeg. Add broth and half and half. Cook and stir until thick and bubbly. In ungreased 2 quart baking dish, layer half of the beans, all the onions and the remaining beans: Spoon sauce over the top. In a medium bowl, toss together bread crumbs, parmesan cheese and oil; sprinkle over vegetables. Bake uncovered for 30-35 minutes or until bubbly. Let stand 10 minutes before serving.

COPPER PENNY CARROTS

2 Lb. Carrots
2 Onions Sliced
1 Green Pepper
1 Can Tomato Soup
1 Cup Vinegar
1 Cup Oil
½ Tsp. Salt
1 Cup Sugar
1 Tsp. Worcestershire Sauce
1 Tsp. Mustard

Thinly slice carrots and cook in boiling salt water for 10 minutes. Drain and cool. Slice onions and separate into rings, slice green pepper into thins strips and combine onions and pepper with carrots. Mix vinegar, salt, Worcestershire sauce, soup, oil, sugar and mustard until well blended.

Then pour over vegetables, stir well, cover and refrigerate overnight.

GINGER GLAZED CARROTS

2 ½ Cups Sliced Carrots
3 Tbsp. Orange Marmalade
2 Tbsp. Butter
1 ½ Tsp. Ginger
3 Tbsp. Orange Juice Concentrate

In a medium saucepan, cook carrots in a small amount of lightly salted boiling water for 3 minutes. Drain and set aside. In the same saucepan, combine preserves, orange juice concentrate, butter and ginger; cook and stir over medium heat until butter is melted. Return carrots to saucepan: Cook, uncovered, over medium heat for 5 minutes or just until carrots are tender and glazed stirring occasionally.

SCALLOPED CORN

2 Cans Cream Style Corn
2 Cups Crushed Crackers
1 Cup Milk
1 Tsp. Salt
½ Cup Grated Onion
1 Tsp. Pepper
2 Eggs Well Beaten
1 Stick Butter

Put milk and corn in pan; add beaten eggs slowly. Add onion and 1 cup of crackers. Stir until hot and pour into greased baking dish. Melt 1 stick of butter and stir in remaining cup of crackers, mixing well. Sprinkle over corn and bake at 350 degrees until brown, about 45 minutes.

FRIED CORN

1 Bag Frozen Corn
3 Tbsp. Bacon Grease
3 Tbsp. Butter
1 Tsp. Salt
1 Tsp. Pepper
1 Cup Water

Place all ingredients in a skillet: cover and bring to a boil, reduce heat and let continue to cook until all water is absorbed. Stir occasionally.

CROCKPOT CORN

20 oz. Frozen Corn
6 Tbsp. Water
½ Stick Butter
8 oz. Cream Cheese Softened

Put all ingredients in the crockpot on low for 3-4 hours. Stir occasionally.

FRENCH-FRIED CAULIFLOWER

1 Head Cauliflower
½ Cup Milk
1 Egg Beaten
1 Tsp. Salt
½ Cup Flour

Break flowerets from cauliflower and cook until tender in salted water. Drain. Beat milk and egg until well blended; dip each floweret into beaten egg-milk mixture and then into bread crumbs mixed with flour. Fry in deep fat until golden brown.

HARVARD BEETS

1 16 oz. Can Sliced Beets
¼ Cup Vinegar
2 Tbsp. Sugar
¼ Tsp. Salt
1 Tbsp. Cornstarch
2 Tbsp. Butter

Drain beets, reserving 1/3 cup liquid. In saucepan combine sugar, cornstarch and salt; stir in reserved beet juice, vinegar and butter. Cook and stir mixture until it thickens. Add beets and cook until heated through.

EGG PLANT SUPREME

1 Lg. Eggplant

1 Jar Spaghetti Sauce
1 Egg
Mozzarella Cheese
2 Cups Cracker Meal
Salt & Pepper to Taste

Slice eggplant 5/8 inch thick. Dip in egg and then in cracker meal mixed with salt and pepper. Fry in hot oil until brown. Remove from skillet and place in casserole dish. Pour spaghetti sauce over eggplant. Top with Mozzarella cheese. Bake in 350 degree oven for approximately 25 minutes or until hot and bubbly.

SCALLOPED POTATOES

6-8 Potatoes Peeled & Sliced
1 Onion Chopped
1 Green Pepper Chopped
3 Cups Bread Crumbs
1 Can Cream Mushroom Soup
1 Cup Velveeta Cubed
1 Can Water
Salt & Pepper to Taste

Peel and slice potatoes and place in a 9x13 pan. Sprinkle with salt and pepper. Cover with onions and peppers. Sprinkle Velveeta over onions and peppers. Mix soup and water and pour Velveeta. Put in 350 degree oven and bake until potatoes are done.

TEXAS POTATOES

2 Lb. Frozen Hash Browns
½ Cup Melted Butter
2 Cup Cheddar Cheese
1 Cup Chopped Onions
1 Can Cream Chicken Soup
1 Tsp. Salt
½ Tsp. Pepper
2 Cups Corn Flakes Crushed
12 oz. Sour Cream

Combine all ingredients except corn flakes, and spoon into a greased 13x9 baking dish. Top with ¼ cup melted butter mixed with crushed corn flakes. Bake at 350 degrees for 45-50 minutes.

OVEN FRIED POTATOES

4-5 Lg. Baking Potatoes
½ Tsp. Garlic Powder
¼ Cup Oil
½ Tsp. Paprika
4 Tbsp. Parmesan Cheese
¼ Tsp. Pepper
1 Tsp. Salt

Do not peel potatoes, wash and cut lengthwise into four wedges. Place skin down in a 13xs9 pan. Combine oil, cheese, salt, garlic powder, paprika and pepper; brush over potatoes. Bake at 375 degrees for 1 hour, brushing with cheese mixture every 15 minutes. Turn potatoes over for last 15 minutes of baking.

SMOKED SAUSAGE & POTATO SKILLET

1 Lb. Smoked Sausage
6-8 Potatoes Peeled & Sliced
¼ Cup Oil
1 Cup Velveeta Cubed
1 Chopped Onion
1 Chopped Green Pepper
Salt & Pepper to Taste
Salsa

In large skillet, heat oil then add potatoes, onions, green pepper, salt and pepper and cook until potatoes are done. Put in a bowl that is lined with paper towels to absorb the grease then return potatoes back to the skillet; add sliced smoked sausage and cook until heated through. Place Velveeta on top, cover with a lid and cook until cheese is melted. Serve with salsa.

SWEET POTATOES

7-8 Sweet Potatoes Peeled
1 Cup Brown Sugar
½ Tsp. Cinnamon
½ Cup Butter
1 Cup Mini Marshmallows

Quarter sweet potatoes then cut in half again, place in saucepan with enough water to cover. Bring to a boil and let cook for about 8-10 minutes. Drain and place in a 13x9 baking dish, dot butter over potatoes, sprinkle with cinnamon and brown sugar. Bake in 350 degree oven for 45 minutes to 1 hour. Put marshmallows on top the last 15 minutes of baking.

SWEET POTATO CASSEROLE

2 Eggs
½ Tsp. Vanilla
1 Cup Sugar
6 Tbsp. Butter
½ Cup Milk
3 Cups Mashed Sweet Potatoes

TOPPING:

1 Cup Brown Sugar
3 Tbsp. Butter
½ Cup Flour
1 Cup Chopped Pecans

Beat eggs; add sugar, butter, vanilla, milk and sweet potatoes. Pour into buttered casserole dish. For topping, mix brown sugar, butter and flour until it looks like cornmeal. Spread on top of sweet potato mixture. Cover with pecans and pat down with hands. Bake at 350 degrees for 45 minutes.

SWEET TATER DELUXE

½ Cup Sugar
¼ Cup Milk
½ Tsp. Salt
3 Tbsp. Butter
½ Tsp. Salt
1 Tsp. Vanilla
2 Large Eggs
4 Cups Mashed Sweet Potatoes

TOPPING

3 Tbsp. Butter
1 Cup Coconut
1 Cup Brown Sugar

1/3 Cup Flour
1 Cup Chopped Pecans

Mix all ingredients and pour into a 9x13 inch pan. Combine all ingredients for topping and sprinkle over potato mixture. Bake at 350 degrees for 35-45 minutes.

BROCCOLI STUFFED POTATOES

4 Large Potatoes
4 Tbsp. Chopped Green Onion
2 Eggs
¼ Tsp. Pepper
½ Cup Sour Cream
1 Cup Chopped Ham
10 oz. Chopped Broccoli
½ Cup Cheddar Cheese

Bake potatoes until done. Slice lengthwise and scoop out potato, leaving ½ inch thick shell. To the potato mixture, mix eggs, sour cream, chopped onion, pepper and ham until blended. Fill shells; top with cooked broccoli, drained. Then sprinkle with shredded cheddar cheese. Bake 20-25 minutes at 400 degrees or until hot.

MUSHROOM BAKE

1 Lb. Fresh Mushrooms
2 Tbsp. Flour
2 Tbsp. Butter
½ Cup Cheddar Cheese Grated
1 Cup Sour Cream
½ Cup Monterey Jack Grated
Dash of Cayenne Pepper

Slice mushrooms in thick slices and sauté in butter until tender. Put in well-buttered baking dish. In saucepan, heat sour cream, flour, salt and pepper to taste; simmer- not boil; Spoon sauce over mushrooms. Mix cheeses together and sprinkle over mushrooms, then sprinkle cayenne pepper over cheese. Bake at 350 degrees for 15-20 minutes.

FAVORITE MUSHROOMS

2 Lg. Pkg. Fresh Mushrooms
Lawry's Salt
8 oz. Shredded Cheddar
Garlic Salt
1/3 Cup Chopped Onion
Lemon Pepper
1 Pkg. Seasoned Croutons
2/3 Stick Butter

Remove stems from mushrooms. Place cap (top side down) in a greased 9x13 pan. Place stems, left over caps, onion, croutons in food processor and chop fine. Add cheese, season to taste. Layer over mushroom caps; drizzle with melted butter and bake at 350 degrees for 30-40 minutes.

CREAMED ONION BAKE

4 Tbsp. Butter
1 ½ Cups Stove Top Stuffing
2 Tsp. Parsley Flakes
3 Cups Sliced Onions
1 Cup Frozen Peas
¼ Cup Milk
1 Cup Shredded Cheddar
1 Can Cream. Mushroom Soup

Melt 2 Tbsp. butter and mix with stuffing mix and parsley; set aside. In medium skillet over medium heat, heat remaining butter; add onions and cook until tender. Stir in soup, milk and peas. Spoon into 2 quart shallow baking dish: Sprinkle with cheese and stuffing mixture over soup mixture; Bake at 350 degrees for 30 minutes or until hot.

FRIED GREEN TOMATOES

4 Green Tomatoes Sliced
1 Cup Milk
1 Egg
1 Cup Flour
1/2 Cup Corn Meal
1 Tsp. Salt
1 Tsp. Pepper
Oil for Frying

In a small bowl whisk together the egg and milk; in another small bowl mix cornmeal, flour, salt and pepper. Heat oil in a large skillet over medium heat; use enough oil to make about ¼ inch depth in skillet. Dip tomato slices first in egg mixture, then in cornmeal mixture. Carefully place slices in hot oil and until browned on both sides.

ZUCCHINI CASSEROLE

6 Cups Sliced Zucchini
1 Sm. Jar Pimentos
8 oz. Sour Cream
3 Crumbled Pieces Bread
1 Chopped Onion
1 Box Stove Top Stuffing
1 Cup Butter Melted
2 Cans Cream Mushroom Soup
2 Shredded Carrots

Cook zucchini until tender; drain. Combine zucchini with pimentos, sour cream, bread crumbs, onion, carrots, ½ cup melted butter and put in 9x13 greased casserole dish. Top with dry dressing mix and remaining ½ cup butter. Bake at 350 degrees for 30-40 minutes.

ITALIAN ZUCCHINI CASSEROLE

2 Medium Zucchini
½ Lb. Cheddar Cheese Cubed
1 Yellow Squash
1 Tsp. Seasoning Salt
1 Small Onion Chopped
1 Tsp. Garlic Powder
15 oz. Can Diced Tomatoes
1 Tsp. Pepper
8 oz. Can Tomato Sauce

Dice the zucchini and squash into 1 inch cubes. Add chopped onion, tomatoes, tomato sauce, cheddar cheese, seasoning salt, garlic powder and pepper. Stir well. Place in casserole dish. Bake in 350 degree oven for 30 – 40 minutes.

-NOTES-

CANDIES AND TREATS

BUCKEYES

2 Lbs. Peanut Butter
3 Lbs. Powdered Sugar
1 Lb. Butter Softened
2-2 ½ Lbs. Almond Bark

Mix peanut butter and butter with mixer. Add powdered sugar and mix well. It gets very hard to mix, so use your hands and mix very, very well. Shape into 1-1 ½ inch balls. Dip each ball into chocolate with toothpick. Don't cover completely so that they will look like a buckeye.

CRISPY CANDY

14 oz. Bag Kraft Caramels
2 Cups Cornflakes
3 Tbsp. Water
4 oz. Coconut
2 Cups Rice Krispies

Melt caramels with water in saucepan over low heat. Stir frequently until sauce is smooth. Pour over combined cereals and coconut until well coated. Drop by rounded spoonful onto greased cookie sheet. Let stand until firm. Makes about 4 dozen

CHOCOLATE COVERED CHERRIES

2 Cans Eagle Brand Milk
2 Tsp. Vanilla
4 Lb. Powdered Sugar
2 Jars Maraschino Cherries
1 Cup Butter

Mix milk, powdered sugar, butter and vanilla together. Form mixture around a cherry. Place balls in freezer overnight. Melt 2 12 oz. packages of chocolate chips with ½ bar of paraffin wax in double boiler (or you can use almond bark). Dip balls in chocolate and place on wax paper.

CHERRY MASH CANDY

2 Cups Sugar
1 Tsp. Vanilla
2/3 Cup Evaporated milk
12 oz. Chocolate Chips
12 Regular Marshmallows
¾ Cup Crunchy Peanut Butter
¼ Cup Butter
6 oz. Cherry Chips
1 Cup Finely Chopped Nuts

Boil in saucepan on medium heat the sugar, milk, marshmallows, and butter for 5 minutes. Remove from heat and stir in cherry chips and vanilla. Pour mixture into a 9x13 buttered pan. Melt the chocolate chips with the butter and add peanut butter and chopped nuts. Stir until well blended, and then pour this mixture on top of the cherry mixture. Let set until cool, and then cut into desired shapes or pieces.

CHOCOLATE CHOW MEIN CLUSTERS

1½ Cups Chocolate Chips
1½ Cups Chow Mein Noodles
1½ Cup Butterscotch Chips
1½ Cups Salted Peanuts

In a heavy saucepan, melt the chocolate and butterscotch chips; stir until smooth. Stir in Chow Mein noodles and the peanuts, mix until coated. Drop by rounded tablespoon onto waxed paper; Makes 2 dozen

CHOCOLATE CARAMEL DRIZZLES

3 Cups Corn Chex
3 Cups Rice Chex
25 Caramels
2 Tbsp. Butter
2 Tbsp. Milk
¼ Cup Chocolate Chips

In large microwavable bowl, mix cereals. In medium microwavable bowl microwave caramels, butter and milk uncovered on high 2 to 3 minutes; stirring after each minute, until caramels are melted and mixture is smooth. Pour over cereals; gently stir until evenly coated; Microwave on high

3 to 4 minutes, stirring after each minute, until just beginning to brown. Spread on waxed paper to cool. In small microwavable bowl, microwave chocolate chips uncovered on high about 1 minute or until chocolate can be stirred smooth. Drizzle over cereal. Refrigerate until set. Store in an air tight container; does not need

CHEX LEMON BUDDIES

9 Cups Rice Chex Cereal
1 ¼ White Chocolate Chips
¼ Cup Butter
4 Tsp. Grated Lemon Peel
2 Tbsp. Lemon Juice
2 Cups Powdered Sugar

In large bowl, measure cereal; set aside. In 1 quart microwavable bowl, microwave chips, butter, lemon peel and juice uncovered on high 1 minute; stir. Microwave about 30 seconds longer or until mixture can be stirred smooth; pour mixture over cereal, stirring until evenly coated. Pour into gallon size zip lock bag, add powdered sugar. Seal bag; gently shake until well coated. Spread on wax paper or foil to cool. Store in air tight container.

PEANUT BUTTER & CHOCOLATE BLAST

6 Cups Rice Chex
1 Cup White Chocolate Chips
1 Cup Peanut Butter Chips
1 Cup Peanut Butter M&M's
1 Cup Dry Roasted Peanuts

Line 2 Cookie sheets with wax paper. Place 3 cups cereal in a large bowl. In a small microwavable bowl, microwave white chocolate chips on high about 1 minute or until chips can be stirred smooth. Pour melted chips over cereal in bowl; stir to evenly coat. Spread mixture in a single layer on one of the cookie sheets. Refrigerate 5 minutes or until set. Repeat the above using the remaining cereal and the peanut butter chips; refrigerate 5 minutes or until set.

Gently break up coated cereal into large bowl. Add candy and peanuts; stir gently to combine.

MUDDY BUDDIES

9 Cups Chex Cereal
1 Cup Chocolate Chips
½ Cup Peanut Butter
¼ Cup Butter
1 Tsp. Vanilla
1 ½ Cups Powdered Sugar

Measure cereal into a large bowl; set aside. In 1 quart microwavable bowl, microwave butter, chocolate chips and peanut butter on high for 1 minute; stir. Microwave about 30 seconds longer or until mixture can be stirred smooth; stir in vanilla. Pour mixture over cereal, stirring until evenly coated. Pour into 2 Gallon zip lock bag. Add powdered sugar; seal bag; shake until well coated. Spread on wax paper to cool Store in an air tight container.

KIBBLES & BITS

3 Cups Cheerios
3 Cups Chex Cereal
1 Cup Pretzels
1 Cup Peanuts
1 Cup M&M's
1 Pkg. White Almond Bark

In a large bowl, combine cereals, pretzels, nuts and M&M's. Melt almond bark in microwave according to directions on package. Pour over cereal mixture and stir until coated. Pour out on wax paper to cook. Break into pieces and store in a sealed container.

CINNAMON CANDY

3 Cups Sugar
1 Tsp. Cinnamon Oil
2 Cups White Syrup
1 Tbsp. Red Food Coloring
1 Cup Water

Heat sugar, syrup and water to hard crack – 300 degrees on thermometer: Remove from heat. Let bubbles disappear and add cinnamon oil and food coloring. Stir and pour onto greased cookie sheet. Let cool and crack into pieces.

FAST FUDGE WREATH

12 oz. Pkg. Chocolate Chips
12 oz. Pkg. Butterscotch Chips
1 Can Eagle Brand Milk
1 Tsp. Vanilla
1 Cup Pecans
1 Jar Maraschino Cherries

Melt chocolate chips, butterscotch chips and eagle brand milk in saucepan on stove. When melted stir in vanilla and nuts. Save some pecans for garnish. Place eagle brand milk can in the center of a pie plate, pour chocolate mixture around can. Garnish with cherries and pecans: Let set until firm.

NEVER FAIL PEANUT BUTTER FUDGE

3 Cups Sugar
½ Tsp. Salt
1 Cup Milnot
1 Stick Butter
1 Tsp. Vanilla
½ Cup Peanut Butter

Mix sugar, Milnot, salt and butter together and cook to soft ball stage. Add peanut butter and vanilla. Mix well and pour into buttered pan. Makes 2 pounds; Cut into small squares.

PEANUT BUTTER FUDGE

1 Pint Marshmallow Crème
2 Cups Sugar
1 Cup Chunky Peanut Butter
2/3 Cup Milk
1 Tsp. Vanilla

Combine marshmallow crème, peanut butter and vanilla in mixing bowl. Then combine sugar and milk in saucepan; cook to soft ball stage; Remove from heat and add peanut butter mixture; beat with mixer and pour into 8x8 pan to set.

RIBBON FANTASY FUDGE

3 Cups Sugar
1-7 oz. Jar Marshmallow Crème
¼ Cup Butter
1 Tsp. Vanilla
2/3 Cup Evaporated Milk
½ Cup Peanut Butter
1-6oz. Pkg. Chocolate Chips

Combine 1 ½ cups sugar, 6 tbsp. butter and 1/3 cup milk in heavy saucepan. Bring to full rolling boil, stirring constantly. Continue stirring 4 minutes over low heat. Remove from heat and stir in chocolate pieces until melted. Add 1 Cup Marshmallow Crème and ½ tsp. vanilla; beat until well blended. Pour into a greased 13x9 pan. Repeat with remaining ingredients, only using peanut butter. Pour over chocolate and cool at room temperature. Cut in squares: Makes 3 pounds.

PEANUT DROP CANDY

¼ Cup Brown Sugar
¾ Cup Peanut Butter
¼ Cup White Sugar
1 Tsp. Vanilla
½ Cup Corn Syrup
2 Cups Rice Krispies

Stir together sugar and syrup in saucepan; bring to a boil; remove from heat. Stir in peanut butter. Mix well. Add vanilla and cereal; stir well. Drop from spoon onto waxed paper: Makes 3 dozen.

PEANUT BRITTLE

4 Tsp. Baking Soda
1 Cup Water
3 Cups Sugar

2 Cups Raw Peanuts
1 Cup White Karo Syrup

Measure baking soda in a cup, mashing lumps; set aside. In a large heavy aluminum pan, put sugar, syrup and water. Boil until soft ball stage on candy thermometer, 240 degrees, stirring frequently. Add peanuts and stir constantly until hard ball stage, 300 degrees. Take off burner and add baking soda. Stir fast because it will foam up. Spread with spoon in two 9x13 inch pans which have been buttered. Let cool; breaks easily.

MICROWAVE PEANUT BRITTLE

1 Cup Raw Peanuts
1 Tsp. Butter
1 Cup Sugar
1 Tsp. Vanilla
½ Cup Corn Syrup
1 Heaping Tsp. Baking Soda
1/8 Tsp. Salt

Combine peanuts, sugar, corn syrup and salt in deep 2 quart bowl. Microwave on high 7-8 minutes, stirring well after 4 minutes: Add butter and vanilla and blend well. Microwave on high for 2 minutes: Gently stir in baking soda until light and foamy. Pour onto buttered cookie sheet. Cool for 1 hour. Break into pieces.

BROWNIE BRITTLE

1 Stick Butter
1 Oz. Unsweetened Chocolate
½ Cup Sugar
¼ Tsp. Vanilla
1 Large Egg
1/3 Cup Flour
½ Cup Crushed Walnuts

Melt butter in a large sauce pan over medium heat. When almost all melted add the chocolate and melt completely. Add the sugar, vanilla and egg, and mix thoroughly until the crystals are the batter very thin and evenly in a 9x9 pan. Bake at 375 degrees for about 20 minutes watching so it doesn't burn. You want it completely baked and almost completely dry to the touch.

MIXED NUT BRITTLE

4 ½ Tbsp. Butter
1 ½ Cups Sugar
1 Cup Water
1 Cup Corn Syrup
10 oz. Mixed Nuts
1 Tsp. Vanilla
1 ½ Tsp. Baking Soda
(Without Peanuts)

Butter a baking sheet with 1 ½ tsp. butter; set aside. In a large saucepan, combine the sugar, water, and corn syrup. Cook over medium heat until a candy thermometer reads 270 degrees (soft-crack stage), stirring occasionally. Add nuts; cook and stir until the mixture reaches 300 degrees (hard-crack stage). Remove from heat and stir in vanilla and remaining butter. Add baking soda and stir vigorously. Quickly pour onto prepared pan. Spread with a buttered spatula to ¼ inch thickness. Cool before breaking into pieces. Makes about 1 ¾ pounds; For Macadamia Almond Brittle use 1 cup each of chopped macadamia nuts and chopped almonds instead of the mixed nuts.

BRICKLE CRUNCH

35 Saltine Crackers
2 Sticks Butter
1 Cup Sugar
1 Cup Chocolate Chips
1 Cup Peanut Butter Chips

PREHEAT oven to 400 degrees. Line a cookie sheet with foil. Lay on cookie sheet, packing tightly. In a medium saucepan, melt butter, and then add sugar and boil, stirring frequently, 2 to 3 minutes, until sugar is completely dissolved. Immediately pour mixture over crackers and bake 7 minutes. Remove from oven and immediately sprinkle chocolate and peanut butter chips over crackers, spreading evenly as they melt.

Refrigerate at least 30 minutes, and then break into pieces. This is great topped with chopped nuts or coconut; just sprinkle either or both on top before refrigerating.

DIVINITY

2 Cups Sugar
1 Tsp. Vanilla
½ Cup Water
2 Egg Whites
½ Cup Corn Syrup

Cook sugar, water and syrup until brittle when dropped into cold water. Beat egg whites and pour in mixture. Beat until it is too thick to beat then turn into a greased pie plate and cut.

NEVER-FAIL DIVINITY

4 Cups Sugar
2 Egg Whites Beaten
1 Cup Water
1 Tsp. Vanilla
1 Cup White Syrup
½ Cup Chopped Black Walnuts

Boil 1 cup sugar and ½ cup water until candy thermometer reaches 238 degrees, soft ball stage. In another pan, boil remaining sugar, syrup and remaining water until thermometer reaches 250 degrees. Slowly pour first sugar mixture over egg whites, beating constantly. Add second mixture and beat until stiff enough to hold shape. Add vanilla and walnuts. Drop by teaspoon on wax paper.

HOLLY CLUSTERS

3 Cups Mini Marshmallows
1 ½ Tsp. Green Food Coloring
1 Stick Butter
4 Cups Corn Flakes
1 Tsp. Vanilla
1 Bag Red Hot's

Melt marshmallows and butter in saucepan; add vanilla and food coloring. Then add corn flakes and mix well until flakes are well coated. Drop mixture on waxed paper with a teaspoon and decorate with red hot's. Let stand until firm.

GRANDMA'S MACAROONS

½ Cup Milk
2 ½ Cups Quick Oats
½ Cup Cocoa
2 Cups Sugar
1 Tsp. Vanilla
1-8 oz. Pkg. Coconut
1 Stick Butter

Boil all ingredients, except coconut, for 1 minute at a rolling boil. Stir in coconut and drop by teaspoon on greased cookie sheet; let cool.

TURTLES

1 Lb. Caramels
½ Cup Corn Syrup
2 Tbsp. Butter
2 Tbsp. Water
1 Tbsp. Water
2 Cups Pecan Halves
1-12 oz. Pkg. Milk Chocolate Chips

Combine over boiling water the caramels, butter and 1 Tbsp. water; heat until caramels melt and mixture is smooth. Keep over boiling water. Combine over hot, not boiling, water the milk chocolate and 2 Tbsp. water and melt until mixture is smooth. Keep warm over hot water. Drop caramel by measuring teaspoons onto greased waxed paper: Place 3 pecan halves on top of each caramel to make head and legs. Drop chocolate mixture over caramel and nuts by slightly-rounded measuring teaspoon. Chill in refrigerator until set, about 30 minutes. Remove from waxed paper onto serving plate. Makes about 4 dozen turtles

MARTHA WASHINGTON CANDY

2 Boxes Powdered Sugar
1 Stick Butter

1 Can Eagle Brand Milk
1 Tsp. Vanilla
¼ Cup Chopped Pecans
1 Cup Coconut
1 Pkg. Chocolate Almond Bark

Cream powdered sugar, butter, milk and vanilla; add nuts and coconut; mix well. Roll into balls the size of a walnut. Use powdered sugar to dip hands in as you roll balls. Dip balls into almond bark that has been melted according to package directions. Drop on waxed paper. Makes about 75 balls.

NEVER FAIL PRALINES

1 Lb. Brown Sugar
3 Tbsp. Butter
1 Cup Milk
1 Cup Chopped Pecans

Mix everything but pecans. Cook until soft ball stage. Remove from heat and beat until thickened. Then add chopped nuts. Drop on waxed paper and place a pecan on each.

O'HENRY BARS

4 Cups Quick Oats
½ Cup Corn Syrup
1 Cup Brown Sugar
1 Cup Chocolate Chips
1 Cup Butter
¾ Cup Peanut Butter

PREHEAT oven to 350 degrees. Mix the oats, brown sugar, butter and corn syrup. Pat into a sheet cake pan and bake for 10-15 minutes. Do not over bake. Melt chocolate chips and peanut butter. Spread over baked crust while hot. Cut into bars right away.

COCONUT BONBONS

½ Cup Butter Softened
2 Lbs. Powdered Sugar

14 oz. Can Eagle Brand Milk
4 Cups Chopped Pecans
10 oz. Flaked Coconut
1 Tsp. Vanilla
2 Cups Chocolate Chips
1 Tbsp. Shortening

In a large mixing bowl cream butter and sugar until light and fluffy; add the milk, pecans, coconut and vanilla; mix well. Shape into 1 inch balls. Refrigerate for 30-45 minutes or until firm. In a heavy saucepan melt the chocolate chips and shortening; stir until smooth. Dip balls and place on waxed paper to set. Store in an airtight container; makes about 21 dozen.

NUTTY CARAMEL CLUSTERS

25 Caramels
1 Tbsp. Butter
1 Tbsp. Milk
1 Cup Sliced Almonds
½ Cup Dry Roasted Peanuts
½ Cup Pecan Halves
½ Cup Chocolate Chips
2 Tsp. Shortening

In 1 qt. microwave bowl, combine the caramels, butter and milk. Microwave, uncovered, on high for 1 ½ - 2 minutes or until caramels are melted, stirring once. Stir in the almonds, peanuts and pecans. Drop by tablespoon on wax paper lined baking sheet. Melt chocolate chips and shortening in the microwave, stir until blended. Spoon over clusters; refrigerate until set. Store in a covered container in the refrigerator.

REESE'S PEANUT BUTTER SQUARES

2 Sticks Butter Melted
1 2/3 Cups Peanut Butter
2 Cups Graham Cracker Crumbs
1 Lb. Powdered Sugar
1-12 oz. Pkg. Chocolate Chips

Mix graham cracker crumbs, melted butter, peanut butter and powdered sugar; press into 9x13 inch pan. Melt chocolate chips and spread over top like frosting. Refrigerate for a few minutes, and then cut into squares.

MAMA'S FUDGE

2 Cups Sugar
4 Tbsp. Cocoa
2/3 Cup Milk
2 Tbsp. Syrup
2 Tbsp. Butter
1 Tsp. Vanilla
¾ Cup Chopped Black Walnuts

In heavy saucepan, combine sugar, cocoa, milk and syrup and bring to a boil, cook to soft ball stage then remove from heat and add butter; beat until lukewarm then add vanilla and nuts. Beat until starting to get thick then spread in buttered 8x8 pan. Cut in squares when cool. I double this and put in 13 x9 pan.

CASHEW CARAMEL FUDGE

2 Tsp. + ½ Cup Butter
7 oz. Marshmallow Crème
1 Can Evaporated Milk
24 Caramels, Quartered
2 ½ Cups Sugar
¾ Cup Cashew Halves
2 Cups Chocolate Chips
1 Tsp. Vanilla

Butter a 9x9 pan with the 2 tsp. butter. In a large saucepan, combine milk, sugar and remaining ½ cup butter. Cook and stir over medium heat until sugar dissolves. Bring to a rapid boil for 5 minutes, stirring constantly. Remove from heat; stir in chocolate chips and marshmallow crème until melted. Fold in caramels, cashews and vanilla; mix well. Pour into prepared pan. Cool. Cut into squares; makes 3 pounds of fudge.

OREO BALLS

1 Pkg. Oreos
8 oz. Soft Cream Cheese

1 Pkg. Almond Bark
Put Oreos in the food processor until you have fine crumbs; mix in cream cheese until well blended. Make into balls and put on cookie sheet. Place in the freezer for about 20 minutes (this makes them easier to handle), dip in melted almond bark and place on waxed paper.

TOFFEE

1 Cup Chopped Pecans
1 ½ Cups Brown Sugar
1 Cup Butter
1 Cup Chocolate Chips

Butter 9x13 pan and sprinkle with pecans. Heat brown sugar and butter to a boil; cook and stir constantly for 7 minutes. Pour over pecans; sprinkle chocolate chips on top and invert cookie sheet over the top and let set for 1-2 minutes; remove the cookie sheet and spread the chocolate chips. Refrigerate until chocolate is set, about 5 minutes, remove from refrigerator and break into pieces (or cut before putting in refrigerator).

CARAMEL CORN

8 Qt. Popped Corn
1 Tsp. Salt
2 Cups Brown Sugar
1 Tsp. Vanilla
2 Sticks Butter
½ Tsp. Baking Soda
½ Cup Karo Syrup

Put popped corn in a large roaster. Put sugar, butter, syrup and salt in a saucepan. Boil 5 minutes. Add vanilla and soda. Pour syrup over corn in roaster. Bake at 200 degrees for 1 hour stirring well every 15 minutes.

POPCORN BALLS

7 Quarts Popped Popcorn
1 Cup Sugar
1 Cup Corn Syrup
¼ Cup Water

¼ Salt
3 Tbsp. Butter
1 Tsp. Vanilla

Place popcorn in a large roaster pan; keep warm in a 200 degree oven. In heavy saucepan, combine the sugar, corn syrup, water and salt. Cook over medium heat until soft ball stage is reached. Remove from heat; add the butter, vanilla; stir until butter is melted. Immediately pour over popcorn and stir until evenly coated. When mixture is cool enough to handle, quickly shape into 3 inch balls, dipping hands in cold water to prevent sticking; Makes 20 popcorn balls

-NOTES-

CANNING

BREAD AND BUTTER PICKLES

12 Large Cucumbers
4 Large Onions
2 Cups Vinegar
3 Cups Water
5 Cups Sugar
1 Tsp. Turmeric
2 Tsp. Mustard Seed
3 Tsp. Celery Seed

Slice cucumbers and onions; soak 4 hours in 4-5 tablespoons of salt and water to cover. Bring to a boil the vinegar, sugar, 3 cups water and spices. Drain cucumbers and onion; put in boiling mixture and cook for 5 minutes. Put in hot scalded jars and seal.

CUCUMBER RELISH

5 Cups Cucumbers
3 Cups Celery
3 Cups Onions
2 Green Peppers
2 Red Peppers
½ Cup Salt
1 ½ Cups Water
2 Tsp. Celery Seed
1 Qt. Vinegar
2 Tsp. Mustard Seed
5 Cups Sugar

Grind cucumbers, celery, onions and peppers. Add salt and water; let stand 10-15 minutes. Drain. Add to drained vegetables the vinegar, sugar, celery seed and mustard seed. Boil for 10 minutes and put in hot scalded jars and seal.

SWEET PEPPER RELISH

12 Sweet Green Peppers
12 Sweet Red Peppers
12 Medium Onions
3 Tbsp. Salt
2 Cups Sugar
2 Cups Vinegar

Grind peppers and onions; place in large bowl. Cover vegetables with boiling water and let stand 5 minutes. Drain. Put vegetables in an enamel pot; add salt, sugar and vinegar. Stir, bring to a boil and continue boiling 5 minutes. Ladle hot mixture into hot jars and seal. Makes 5 pints

CORN RELISH

2 Qt. Cut Corn
1 Tbsp. Mustard Seed
1 Cup Chopped Onion
1-2 Cups Sugar
1 Qt. Chopped Cabbage
1 Tbsp. Celery Seed
1 Cup Sweet Red Pepper
1 Tbsp. Salt
1 Cup Sweet Green Pepper
1 Tbsp. Turmeric
2 Tbsp. Dry Mustard
1 Cup Water
1 Qt. Vinegar

Cut corn off the cob and chop the peppers. Combine all ingredients in a large pot and bring to a boil. Turn down and simmer for 20 minutes. Pour into hot, scalded, jars and seal.

CHOW-CHOW RELISH

1 Qt. Chopped Cabbage
2 Tsp. Celery Seed
2 Cups Chopped Onion
3 Cups Chopped Cauliflower
2 Cups Sweet Green Pepper
2 Cups Green Tomatoes
1 Cup Sweet Red Peppers
3 Tbsp. Salt
2 ½ Cup Vinegar
1 ½ Cups Sugar
2 Tsp. Dry Mustard
1 Tsp. Ground Ginger
1 Tsp. Mustard Seed

Chop peppers and tomatoes; combine all the vegetables and sprinkle with salt. Let stand 4-6 hours in a cool place. Drain well. Combine vinegar, sugar and spices; simmer 10 minutes. Bring to boiling. Ladle into hot jars and seal. You can add hot peppers if you want to make hot chow- chow.

CUCUMBER OR ZUCCHINI RINGS

1 Gal. Rings
6 Sticks Cinnamon
½ Cup White Vinegar
1 Cup Lime
½ oz. Red Food Coloring
1 Gal. Water
1 ½ Tsp. Alum
1 ½ Cups White Vinegar
7 ½ Cups Sugar
1 ½ Cups Water
9 ½ oz. Red hot's

Use big cucumbers and cut ½ inch thick. Peel and slice. Cut center out to remove seeds. Mix 1 cup lime with 1 gallon water; pour over and soak 24 hours. Drain and wash well. Soak in clear ice water for 3 hours. Mix ½ cup vinegar, food coloring, alum and water enough to cover cucumbers; simmer. Then let stand for 2 hours. Drain. Mix 1 ½ cups of vinegar, sugar, 1 ½ cups of water, cinnamon and red hot's; bring to a boil. Pour over pickle rings and let set overnight. Pour off syrup and reheat for 3 mornings. Third day, heat rings in syrup, put in jars and seal.

PEACH BUTTER

1 Gallon Peach Pulp
8 Cups Sugar

To prepare pulp, wash, pit and peel peaches. Chop peaches. Cook until soft, adding only enough water to prevent sticking. Press through a sieve or food mill. Add sugar and cook until thick, about 30 minutes. As mixture thickens, stir frequently to prevent sticking. Pour hot into hot jars and seal.

PEAR BUTTER

1 Gallon Pear Pulp

8 Cups Sugar
2 Tsp. Grated Orange Rind
2/3 Cup Orange Juice
1 Tsp. Nutmeg

To prepare pulp, peel, quarter and core pears; cook until soft, adding only enough water to prevent sticking. Press through a sieve or food mill and measure pulp. Add remaining ingredients and cook until thick, about 15-20 minutes. As mixture thickens, stir frequently to prevent sticking. Pour in jars and seal.

CROCK-POT APPLE BUTTER

5 Lbs. Apples
4 Cups Sugar
3 Tsp. Cinnamon
¼ Tsp. Cloves
¼ Tsp. Salt

Peel, core and chop apples; place in a bowl and pour sugar, cinnamon, cloves and salt over apples and mix well. Place in crock pot, cover and cook on high 1 hour. Decrease heat to low and continue cooking for 7-9 hours stirring occasionally. Whisk to make sure it is smooth then ladle into jars and seal.

APPLE SAUCE

12 Cups Apples
½ Tsp. Cloves
1 Cup Water
1 Cup Sugar
1 Tsp. Cinnamon

Peel, core and chop the apples; place in a large pot and combine with water cinnamon and cloves. Bring to a boil, reduce heat and simmer for 10 minutes. Stir in sugar and simmer 5 more minutes. Put in jars and seal.

PEACH BUTTER

4-5 Lbs. Peaches
½ Cup Water

4 Cups Sugar
1 Tbsp. Cinnamon (Optional)

Wash peaches, remove seeds and any bad spots-DO NOT PEEL! Chop peaches. Put in large pot with ½ cup water and cook over medium heat until peaches are soft, about 15-20 minutes depending on the ripeness of your fruit. Run the peaches through a food mill or sieve; discard the skins. You should have about 2 quarts of pulp. Mix pulp with sugar and cinnamon, cook over medium heat until thick, 30- minutes to 1 hour. Stir frequently to prevent sticking. Place in hot jars and seal.

BLACKBERRY JAM

5 Cups Crushed Blackberries (Use Potato Masher)
7 Cups Sugar
1 Tsp. Butter
1 Pkg. Sure Jell

Carefully measure out berries, put them in a very large pot. Measure the sugar into a large bowl. Add the Sure Jell to the berries a little at a time, stirring constantly. Add butter and heat on high, stirring constantly until mixture comes to a full boil; add sugar all at once; stir. Bring mixture back to a full hard boil stirring constantly. Boil for 1 minute; remove from heat and ladle into clean, hot jars and seal.

STRAWBERRY JAM

5 Cups Crushed Strawberries (Crush with Potato Masher)
7 Cups Sugar
 1 Pkg. Sure Jell
½ Tsp. Butter

Carefully measure out berries, put them in a very large pot. Measure the sugar into a large bowl. Add the Sure Jell to the berries a little at a time, stirring constantly. Add butter and heat on high, stirring constantly until mixture comes to a full boil; add sugar all at once; stir. Bring mixture

back to a full hard boil stirring constantly. Boil for 1 minute; remove from heat and ladle into clean, hot jars and seal.

ZUCCHINI JELLY

7 Cups Grated Zucchini
7 Cups Sugar
1 Can Crushed Pineapple
2 Boxes Apricot Jell-O

Put zucchini and sugar into a large pot and bring to a boil; boil for 7 minutes. Add the pineapple and return to a boil for 7 more minutes. Remove from heat and add the Jell-O, stir until well blended. Put in jars and seal.

SALSA

10 Cups Chopped Peeled Fresh Tomatoes
3 Cups Chopped Green Bell Pepper
5 Cups Chopped Onion
1 ½ -2 ½ Cups Jalapeno Peppers Chopped, Seeded
1 ¼ Cups Cider Vinegar
3 Cloves Garlic Minced
2 Tbsp. Cilantro Minced
3 Tsp. Salt

Combine all ingredients in a large pot; bring to a boil, turn down and simmer to desired thickness. Put in jars and seal. (Put a few peppers at a time until desired hotness is reached).

CANNED TOMATOES

Peeled Fresh Tomatoes
Canning Salt

To peel tomatoes cover them with hot water and let set a few minutes, skins will slide right off. Remove core and quarter (or leave whole) and place in pot. Bring to a boil and continuing cooking until tomatoes are hot through. Put in jars add 1 Tsp. of canning salt to each quart, seal.

TOMATO JUICE

Tomatoes
Canning Salt

Put tomatoes in food processor and blend well. Rub through a sieve; this will remove all seeds and skins. Put pulp and juice in a large pot and bring to a boil. Boil for 3-4 minutes; pour in quart jars and add 1 Tsp. canning salt to each quart. May add hot peppers if you want hot tomato juice. Or you can add bell peppers, onions and celery to tomatoes in the food processor to make V-8 Juice.

-NOTES-

-ADDITIONAL NOTES -

INGREDIENT SUBSTITUTIONS

WHEN YOU NEED	IN THIS AMOUNT	SUBTITUTE
Baking Powder	1 teaspoon	½ teaspoon of tartar plus ¼ teaspoon baking soda
Broth	1 cup	1 cup hot water plus 1 teaspoon bouillon granules or 1 bouillon cube
Buttermilk	1 cup	1 tablespoon lemon juice or vinegar plus enough milk to measure 1 cup; let stand 5 minutes. Or 1 cup plain yogurt
Cajun Seasoning	1 teaspoon	¼ teaspoon cayenne pepper. ½ teaspoon dried thyme, ¼ teaspoon dried basil and 1 minced garlic clove
Chocolate, Semisweet	1 square (1 ounce)	1 square (1 once) unsweetened chocolate plus 1 tablespoon sugar or 3 tablespoons semisweet chocolate chips
Chocolate	1 square (1 ounce)	3 tablespoons baking cocoa plus 1 tablespoon shortening or vegetable oil
Cornstarch (for thickening)	1 tablespoon	2 tablespoon all-purpose flour
Corn Syrup, Dark	1 cup	¾ cup light corn syrup plus ¼ cup molasses
Corn Syrup, Light	1 cup	1 cup sugar plus ¼ cup water
Cracker Crumbs	1 cup	1 cup dried bread crumbs
Cream, Half-and Half	1 cup	1 tablespoon melted butter plus enough whole milk to measure 1 cup
Egg	1 whole	2 egg whites or 2 egg yolks or ¼ cup egg substitute
Flour, Cake	1 cup	1 cup minus 2 tablespoon (7/8 cup) all-purpose flour
Flour, Self-Rising	1 cup	1 cup all-purpose flour plus 1 teaspoon baking powder, ½ teaspoon salt and ¼ teaspoon baking soda
Garlic, Fresh	1 clove	1/8 teaspoon garlic powder
Gingerroot, Fresh	1 teaspoon	¼ teaspoon ground ginger
Honey	1 cup	1-1/4 cups sugar plus ¼ cup water
Lemon Juice	1 teaspoon	¼ teaspoon cider vinegar
Lemon Peel	1 teaspoon	½ teaspoon lemon extract
Milk, Whole	1 cup	½ cup evaporated milk plus ½ cup water or 1 cup water plus 1/3 cup nonfat dry milk powder
Molasses	1 cup	1 cup honey
Mustard, Prepared	1 tablespoon	½ teaspoon ground mustard plus 2 tablespoons vinegar
Onion	1 small (1/3 cup chopped0	1 teaspoon onion powder or 1 tablespoon dried minced onion
Poultry Seasoning	1 teaspoon	¾ teaspoon rubbed sage plus ¼ teaspoon dried thyme
Sour Cream	1 cup	1 cup plain yogurt
Tomato Juice	1 cup	½ cup tomato sauce plus ½ cup water
Tomato Sauce	2 cups	¾ cup tomato paste plus 1 cup water
Yeast	1 package (1/4 once) active dry	1 cake (5/8-ounce) compressed yeast

FOOD EQUIVALENTS

FOOD	EQUIVALENTS
Apples	1 pound (3 medium) = 2-3/4 cups sliced
Apricots	1 pound (8 to 12 medium) = 2-1/2 cups sliced
Bananas	1 pound (3 mediums) = 1-1/3 cups mashed or 1-1/2 to cups sliced
Berries	1 pint = 1-1/2 cups to 2 cups
Bread	1 loaf = 16 to 20 slices
Bread Crumbs	1 slice = ½ cup soft crumbs or ¼ cup dry crumbs
Butter or margarine	1 pound = 2 cups or 4 sticks / 1 stick = 8 tablespoons
Cheese	
Cottage	1 pound = 2 cups
Shredded	4 ounces = 1 cup
Cherries	3-½ cups halved
Chocolate Chips	6 ounces = 1 cup
Cocoa, Baking	1 pound = 4 cups
Coconut, Flacked	14 ounces = 5-1/2 cups
Cornmeal	1 pound = 3 cups uncooked
Corn Syrup	16 ounces = 2 cups
Cranberries	12 ounces = 3 cups whole or 2-1/2 cups finely chopped
Cream Cheese	8 ounces = 16 tablespoons
Cream, Whipping	1 cup = 2 cups whipped
Dates, Dried	1 pound = 2-3/4 cups Pitted and chopped
Dates, Dried and Chopped	10 ounces = 1-3/4 cups
Egg Whites	1 cup = 8 to 10 whites
Flour	
All-Purpose	1 pound = about 3-1/2 cups
Cake	1 pound = about 4-1/2 cups
Whole Wheat	1 pound = about 3-3/4 cups
Frozen Whipped Topping	8 ounces = 3-1/2 cups
Peaches	1 pound (4 medium) = 2-3/4 cups sliced

FOOD	EQUIVALENTS
Gelatin, Unflavored	1 envelope = tablespoon
Graham Crackers	16 crackers = 1 cup crumbs
Grapefruit	1 medium = ¾ cup juice or 1-1/2 cups segments
Grapes	1 pound = 3 cups
Honey	1 pound = 1-1/3 cups
Lemons	1 medium = 3 tablespoons juice or 2 teaspoon grated peel
Limes	1 medium = 2 tablespoon juice or 1-1/2 teaspoons grated peel
Marshmallows	
Large	1 cup = 7 to 9 marshmallows
Miniature	1 cup = about 100 marshmallows
Nectarines	1 pound (3 medium) = 3 cups sliced
Nuts	
Almonds	1 pound = 3 cups halves or 4 cups slivered
Ground	3-3/4 ounces = 1 cup
Hazelnuts	1 pound = 3-1/2 cups whole
Pecans	1 pound = 4-1/2 cups chopped
Walnuts	1 pound = 3-3/4 cups chopped
Oats	
Old-Fashioned	1 pound = 5 cups
Quick-cooking	1 pound = 5-1/2 cups
Oranges	1 medium = 1/3 to ½ cups juice or 4 teaspoons grated peel
Pears	1 pound (3 medium) = 3 cups sliced

FOOD	EQUIVALENTS
Pineapples	1 medium = 3 cups chunks
Popcorn	1/3 to ½ cup unpopped = 8 cups popped
Rhubarb	1 pound = 3 cups chopped (raw) or 2 cups (cooked)
Yeast, Active	1 envelope = 2-1/4 teaspoon

FOOD	EQUIVALENT
Raisins	15 ounces = 2-1/2 cups
Shortening	1 pound = 2 cups
Strawberries	1 pint = 2 cups hulled and sliced
Sugar	
Brown Sugar	1 pound = 2-1/4 cups
Confectioner's Sugar	1 pound = 4 cups
Granulated	1 pound = 2-1/4 to 2-1/2 cups

To order additional books:

Beacon of Hope Ministries
P.O. BOX 258
Cameron, Missouri 64429
Or

Beaconofhopemin.org
Click on Bible Truths Restored Publications
you may e-mail us @ bohmin17@yahoo.com
Follow us on Facebook

Made in the USA
Columbia, SC
10 August 2019